Divination

the Search for Meaning

COMPASS OF MIND

Knowledge is a dangerous thing, as Adam and Eve found out in the Garden of Eden. Yet without it, humanity would not evolve. Knowledge leads to new pathways of understanding, shaping our views of the world and extending our ability to create. Sometimes ways in which to apply knowledge are sought; at others, knowledge itself is enough, for it is said that man is made in the image of God, and, through knowing himself, can know the divine.

The series "Compass of Mind" is founded in this view of an integrated physical, human and spiritual universe. It looks at various ways in which knowledge is discovered and formulated, drawing themes from mystical and esoteric traditions, from the creative arts, and from therapies and broad-based science. For each topic the questions are posed: "What kind of a map of the world is this?" and "What special insights does it bring?" The series title embodies the concept that knowledge begins and ends with mind; a question asked expands into a circle which is both defined and investigated by mind itself.

Authors of "Compass of Mind" titles bring a wide perspective and a depth of personal experience to their chosen themes. Each text is written with clarity and sympathy, attractive to the lay reader and specialist alike. Themes are illustrated with lively, well-researched examples, aimed at revealing the essence of the subject, for these are books which tackle the question of "Why?" rather than "How to?"

Cherry Gilchrist, series editor

DIVINATION
the search for meaning

CHERRY GILCHRIST

DRYAD PRESS LIMITED
LONDON

First published 1987
Typeset by
Latimer Trend & Company Ltd,
Plymouth
Printed by Biddles Ltd,
Guildford,
Surrey
for the publishers
Dryad Press Limited,
8 Cavendish Square,
London W1M 0AJ

ISBN 0 8521 9697 0

CONTENTS

Chapter 1 Divination – The Gateway to Knowledge 7
Chapter 2 Images of Change 22
Chapter 3 The Tarot – The Symbolic Circus 54
Chapter 4 Questions and Answers 81
Chapter 5 Approaching Divination 99
Chapter 6 Creating Systems 114
Chapter 7 "The Truth about Time" 130

Some Suggested Reading 151
Index 157

Acknowledgment

The cover illustration is by Gila Zur.

Chapter 1

Divination – The Gateway to Knowledge

To divine is to journey into the unknown. Divination involves travelling beyond the limits of ordinary, rational knowledge into a realm where we may discover knowledge not usually accessible to us. We hope there to catch a glimpse of what is, what has been and what will be. The world into which divination leads is full of meaning, even though it may be strange to us. We dare to venture into it because we can sense that meaning underlying the jumble of everyday impressions and encounters; we can sense that our normal perceptions of time and events are limited, describing only the outlines of a three-dimensional reality. Divination is one means of coming to know this reality, which we may experience as a sense of greater order and significance running through our lives. Divination, in its truest sense, is to know the divine.

The realm that we enter through divination is mysterious, and taxes our normal mode of understanding. And yet we can discern some of its features, and the principles from which it is created. In this book I shall be suggesting ways in which we can describe and define these, in the hope that both those who already practise divination and those who are learning about it for the first time will find some light shed on the process of divination itself. Divination is a topic often treated with hazy reverence, superstition, or downright scepticism. Much of the ignorance and undue awe surrounding divination could be dispelled through looking at its principles and implications, rather than just at its results, and it is this line of enquiry that I shall pursue in the present work. Divination cannot be considered separately from religious and cultural world views, nor from those who practise it. The method of divination chosen, the context in which it is used, and the person who applies it are all essentially interrelated, and will determine the kind of results obtained.

However sound the integrity of the diviner, and however skilful the techniques applied, though, divination remains uncertain in terms of results. There is no guarantee that it will be right every time. The conditions in which we approach divination are very important – our frame of mind, the nature of the question, its timing, and the method used are all relevant. This is why so many ceremonies and rituals have built up around divination. Some of these can seem absurd or superstitious if looked at in isolation, and, like all aids, can be more of a hindrance than a help if one can no longer operate without them. But the underlying intention is to create special conditions which help to set divination apart from mundane activities. The diviner tries to become detached from normal distractions and considerations, and attempts to go beyond the constraints of rational logic into a level of consciousness where a kind of "super-logic" can be perceived.

Later in this book I shall be going in more depth into the subject of preparations for divination, and also suggesting ways in which we can begin to make sense of the world into which divination precipitates us, for it is more fluid in form, more spacious and more potent than our everyday world. Time there appears to be more than a linear sequence of past, present and future. Simple questions have a habit of revealing complexity; complex questions may be reduced to a heartening simplicity. Events that seemed casual take their place, with dazzling clarity, as part of a pattern, and a humdrum life may reveal itself to be imbued with destiny.

These may seem grandiose claims for divination. Divination can, after all, be no more than rolling a few dice or discovering underground water. It can become a party trick, a children's game, or an outdated superstition. Yet I hope I shall be able to show that there are connections between all these and the *core practice* of divination, which is a way of knowledge. As the old masters of divination and philosophy hastened to tell us, knowledge can derive from many different levels, giving understanding of the natural, human or divine worlds.

The divinatory methods used are usually tailored to suit the information being sought, and require varying complexity of technique and skill. Whether the method is straightforward or complicated, the responsibility of the diviner always remains paramount. He or she must act as interpreter and as communicator, for the knowledge gained has to be put into a form and conveyed with consideration for the recipient. Of course, there are differing degrees of responsibility; someone trying to predict the winner of the Grand National through numerology does not have the same consideration of judgement as a palmist asked to read a client's character and life pattern. The fact that the knowledge gained through divination can be interpreted in different ways and conveyed with different nuances of meaning, however, makes the work of divination all the more taxing. The diviner acts as a bridge between worlds, bringing knowledge through in a form that we can understand.

Before outlining any particular practices, I would like to suggest an image to represent the whole basic process of divination. Such a picture may be useful in recognising the different stages of the process and the phenomena we encounter. It is only one viewpoint, for maps and symbols are never absolute, although they can be extremely effective in opening up areas of understanding.

An Image of Divination

There is a circular walled garden, of immense size and variety, and in its centre a squarely-built tower. The tower has at least four doors, but a key is needed to open any one of them. On entering the tower, the first impression is of darkness and, perhaps, of bats or scuttling creatures. There are empty corners, where there is nothing but a bleak and hollow space. But within the fortress there is a circular chamber, and here three figures stand around a large brazier, whose ornate lid may be lifted off to reveal a bright flame. The watchers are attentive and steady, studying the fire's lively movement and the curling of the smoke. Deeper in the heart of the tower is yet another room, and it is as though this is reached only by passing through the fire in the brazier. In this chamber there are also watchers, but they are silent and receptive, gazing at a central light which is full of life but devoid of form. This same light, almost like a basic pulse of energy, also surrounds the garden outside the tower; it is both the outermost and the innermost.

The garden represents our normal environment. There is plenty for us to do and enjoy in the garden, since it is always changing, growing, decaying. Most of the time we do not question the pattern of events there, as they are self-explanatory. Sometimes, however, these events seem out of the ordinary; or it is as if something has been thrown in over the wall from outside; or a burning question arises to which nothing in the garden can provide an answer. The search for meaning that follows leads us to the tower, where divination shows us the door by which to enter. To open the door a key is needed; this key is the method used, and to turn it in the lock requires well-focused intention. Once inside, if the intention is not clear or strong enough, the seeker may be repelled by the figments of imagination that fly at him (the bats and creatures of the dark), or even mistake them for the objective truth. Similarly, he or she may come across the empty dark spaces and turn away despondently, convinced that there is nothing to be found and that the only reality is in the garden outside. If the diviner penetrates to the chamber with the brazier, then the seeker becomes the watcher. The living flame is meaning, and in the fire and smoke he or she will try to decipher that meaning, which is itself an ever-changing and moving state. In divination this will be done through the particular language of the practice, the interplay of symbols or numbers for instance. The diviner actively endeavours to discern the qualities and forms in the flame and to turn them into human language, aided by the medium of the divinatory code. To go to the innermost chamber is not strictly necessary for divination purposes, but it is certainly desirable to know that it is there. This is the manifestation of truth itself, which in its primal state has no form but great potency. It could also be called the divine source of life, as it lies both at the heart and at the perimeter of the kingdom. It is advisable for the diviner to recognise this source, without which there would be no succession of forms to perceive, no personal volition, no communicable knowledge. However far a diviner penetrates into meaning, he or she never has the final answer.

In the terms of this image, then, divination is the practice of entering the tower with purpose, seeking the fire of knowledge, transforming it into understandable language, and bringing the discoveries back out into the light of day. Although, as I stress, it is only one way of describing the process, the picture will be useful to keep in mind, as I shall relate various aspects of divination directly to it in later chapters. It also serves as a reminder that there is a "blueprint" for divination. In other words, it is easy to become confused when faced with a mass of divinatory practices, from folk superstitions to prophetic oracles, and to lose sight of the link between them. Although there are wide variations of method, and also of depth, there is a common thread, which this symbol helps to portray. The basic aim is neatly encapsulated in the *Concise Oxford Dictionary*: "Divination – Divining: insight into or discovery of the unknown or future by supernatural means" and "Supernatural: . . . due to manifesting some agency above the forces of nature, outside the ordinary operation of cause and effect".

Divination in the Life of Mankind

To make a complete classification of divination practices throughout history and in all cultures would be a task of major proportions. Divination in one form or another seems to have been a feature of just about every society on record. In Babylonia at least four thousand years ago the priests were at work noting and interpreting eclipses of sun and moon, and their predictions were considered to have vital significance for the country's ruler and economy. The Greeks visited their famous oracle at Delphi, where the pronouncements of the Pythia, the appointed priestess, were communicated by her priests to the anxious enquirer. Celts in pagan Britain looked to birds for omens, judging their cries and flight as portents of events to come. And, of course, there are famous examples of divination in the Bible, such as the episode where Joseph interprets Pharaoh's dream, predicting the fat and the lean years that were to come for Egypt.

Among primitive and peasant societies divination has been as prominent as in more sophisticated cultures. If such practices were properly studied, they would probably reveal themselves to be as effective, though perhaps not as complex, as systems of divination requiring written words and numbers. In tribal societies, dreams, for instance, are acknowledged as a source of divinatory information, and there is nothing to suggest that the dreams of an American Indian or a Laplander are any less subtle than our own. In fact, in some cases, these people seem to have developed to a high degree the skills of recalling, interpreting, and perhaps even of invoking dreams. According to Fraser (*The Golden Bough*), a Lapp woman in pregnancy was expected to divine through a dream the name and identity of a dead ancestor whose spirit would be born again in her child. Divination in tribal societies is often a specialist occupation taken up by a shaman, or shaman-type figure, who would use his or her powers of vision, dreaming and augury to solve mysteries and answer questions about the future. Sometimes these official diviners were established as part of a prominent cult; a Norse saga records that a company of nine seeresses travelled from place to place in Greenland offering their services as oracles, acting under the authority of the goddess Freya.

Geographically and historically, therefore, divination has been as widespread an activity as any religious or social custom. In the West today it has not lost its purpose or popularity, although the general acceptance of divination certainly fluctuates. Writing a book on the subject of divination would have been considered an interesting and enlightening project between late Victorian times and the 1920s, and a literary curiosity or even an eccentric idea between then and the 1960s, when a revival of all things mysterious and esoteric began. Nevertheless, there is an unbroken thread of interest in divination running throughout our history, even though its outer image has waxed and waned. Divination is not a cultural aberration, or a past phase of human evolution. It is a living tradition.

The Scope of Divination

The practice of divination implies that there is a question to ask, and a diviner or interpreter to apply a divinatory method. The questioner and the diviner may be one and the same person, and we will look more closely at the nature of the diviner in a later chapter, in terms of who this might be, and the kinds of skills and qualities needed. Likewise, the answers to divination, and their significance, will be considered further on. For the moment, I will attempt to give an overview of the scope of divination, an outline which will be expanded in due course. Such an outline helps to set the parameters of this book; it is not a final definition of divination. Indeed, the boundaries of divination are hard to fix, since it is difficult to know when it runs into another field of operation – clairvoyance or psychoanalysis, for instance. And to classify all its practices would be a lifetime's work in itself. What I hope to do here is to delineate some of the basic components of divination, the focal points around which most practices cohere.

Divination starts with a question. There is something that one wishes to know. And, usually, it is knowledge that one cannot gain by ordinary means. Asking questions about the future is one of the most common lines of divinatory enquiry, and it is sometimes assumed that this encompasses the whole of divination. It is also this type of enquiry that provokes the most controversy, for it brings up uncomfortable questions of fate and free will, and the dilemma of whether we may and should know what will come to pass. The questioner may ask, "What is going to happen?", but also "What will happen if I do so and so?" This latter form of questioning – preferred, incidentally, by the Delphic oracle – has a different bias to it, for it implies that a choice made in the present will have consequences in the future, and that these consequences can be revealed by divination.

Divination may also be concerned with the past. The querent may want to know, "What did happen?" Such questions were favourites in seventeenth-century England, where an outraged householder would consult a horary astrologer to find out who had abducted his best cow or carried off the family silver. It is easily seen, from this, that divinatory questions concerning the past can have a very practical application! Psychometrists specialise in "reading" the past history of objects through touch, or the character of their owners. Questions based on the present also have a place. "Is she presently at home?" (before the days of telephones!), "Has he got another girlfriend?" and "Where is my missing ring?" are also quite explicit in purpose. It is perhaps worth pointing out at this stage that both the mundane questions and the profound ones are all part of the compass of divination, and each type can illustrate different aspects of the process. In fact, even discerning whether a question *is* superficial can be tricky, since an apparently trivial query may have great significance to a questioner, whereas a request for personal guidance, if put as a passing fancy, may draw forth very little of illumination. Certain methods of divination have built-in safeguards so that, in fact, they do not operate if the relationship between the querent, enquiry and diviner is not well-balanced. Others depend upon preliminary rituals, or are only performed on certain occasions, thus deterring casual or constant questioning. Perhaps, though, a minor or amusing question should not be thought of as out of the proper sphere of divination. To divine is to seek for knowledge, and human curiosity prompts us to ask all sorts of questions.

As well as asking questions which relate specifically to past, present and future, the enquirer may also want to investigate areas which relate to states of being. The most obvious example of this is a request for a character-reading, often divined through palmistry, physiognomy, or mainstream astrology. Divination is concerned with the quest for self-knowledge. It is often asked of astrologers: What is the point of giving character descriptions, since most of us think we know our own natures pretty well? Apart from the fact that we tend to overlook certain little traits of personality, and may not have quite the same view of ourselves as others do, such a reading can create a powerful impression. It seems to reveal the blueprint upon which we have constructed our life, to show the archetypal qualities of our nature, and to connect up apparently random characteristics into a bigger scheme. Far from being a narcissistic indulgence, a character-reading can lead to a sense of our own place in a universal ordering. Cornelius Agrippa, a famous occult philosopher of the sixteenth century, explained it thus:

> God also created man after his image; for as the world is the image of God, so man is the image of the world. . . . Whosoever therefore shall know himself, shall know all things in himself; especially he shall know God, according to whose image he was made; he shall know the world, the resemblance of which he beareth; he shall know all creatures, with which he symbolizeth . . . and how all things may be fitted for all things, in their time, place, order, measure, proportion and Harmony. (*Of Occult Philosophy*: Book Three)

Although divinatory questions are usually posed in connection with personal affairs, it is also feasible to ask about a third party, where ethics permit. In its history, divination has been used to ask questions about almost every aspect of life, from the weather to politics, from missing animals to theological riddles. In theory, at least, it seems that a certain amount of information or knowledge can be gleaned through using any one of a variety of divinatory techniques, though the attitude and method used have to be tempered to the scope of the question. Intention is all-important in divination.

The subjects most commonly enquired about through divination are love, money, health and children. This is hardly surprising, since they are at the forefront of human concern and can be the most capricious and unpredictable in their manifestations. There is also an important strand of divination which is connected with the location of objects. "Objects" is used very loosely here, and can cover creatures, persons and substances.

Divining for substances, sometimes known as "dowsing", is an ancient art, known in Europe at least as early as the Renaissance. It seems to have been introduced into England by German miners during the reign of Queen Elizabeth. With a rod, forked stick, pendulum or even bare hands, the diviner aims to locate water or minerals, metals, and other buried substances, and through particular techniques their depth and quantity can also be estimated. The success rate of these types of diviners is good enough for them to be employed by water boards and mining companies. Dowsing can also be extended into the hunt for lost articles, people or animals.

There is an argument that dowsers are using a very sensitive form of physical perception, picking up, for instance, on the presence of water nearby and translating tiny impulses of response into marked and noticeable movements with a divining rod. While there may be truth in this, it is also true that certain of these diviners can work equally well from maps, and do not need to be in the actual location that is being searched. To grapple with the mysteries of divining, we need to extend our normal concept of human senses and abilities. Perhaps dowsers do work from their physical senses – dowsing is certainly a very different operation from, say, reading the Tarot cards – but perhaps, also, physical responses can be induced to work in an imaginary replica of the location. A map is literally an image of a terrain. And images and symbols, as will be discussed, are an intrinsic part of divination.

Evolution in Divination

Although it is not easy to chart historical changes in divination, it is probably true to say that there has been a move away from collective purposes for divination to individual ones. In the early days of astrology, for instance, most predictions were concerned with the future of the king or emperor, on whose well-being the whole nation was thought to depend; or with wars, plagues and harvests that would affect the common good. Around the dawning of the Christian era, the Greeks set up astrology on a more individual basis, and the personal horoscope then became the main focus of astrology. Naturally, political affairs are still a matter of interest to us, and political divination is encompassed by the practice of "mundane" astrology, but it seems that we do not nowadays place so much emphasis on the well-being of a leader or sovereign, or make our first priority that of divining on a collective basis. In societies where the collective identity is felt to be stronger than the individual identity – that is to say, when a person's prime sense of well-being derives from the state of his tribe or country rather than from his own affairs – then divination tends to centre upon general, social issues.

Historical changes in the divinatory methods chosen are not strongly marked. However, there are some practices which are definitely out of fashion. One of the clearest examples of this is augury by means of entrails. Popular in Biblical, Babylonian and Roman times, it required the slaughter of a chosen beast, perhaps a sheep or a cockerel, whose insides would be examined for distinguishing marks or features. The liver was a popular organ for inspection, and some texts in the library of Assurbanipal, King of Assyria, where the cuneiform texts of Ninevah were collected, gave the prescribed interpretations for its individual conformations. (In the following quotation parts of, and marks on, the liver are indicated by terms with initial capital letters.)

There is a Place, the Road is double. That on the right crosses that on the left. The enemy will rage with his weapons against those of the prince. . . . A Finger is placed on the right side of the Place: ruin of the army or of the sanctuary.

The left part of the Bitter is closed: your foot crushes the enemy. The lower face of the liver bears lesions on the right: lesion of the head, change plan of campaign.

(Quoted by Jack Lindsay in *Origins of Astrology*, Muller, 1971)

It will, I hope, suffice to give one example of entrail divination, as it is certainly not a practice found in the mainstream of Western divination today.

The drawing of lots, especially to determine right and wrong, has largely faded from sight. This may be due to several factors. For instance, we now have complex legal procedures and are not encouraged to take the law into our own hands, a different situation from the days when communities were more isolated and policemen unknown. Secondly, the ferocious witch hunts of the seventeenth century, resulting in thousands of executions based on spurious evidence and divination procedures (a "guilty" witch would float, whereas an "innocent" woman would drown), have left a lasting scar; wisely, or otherwise, we are now wary of deciding questions of right and wrong, or of guilt and innocence. But there are plenty of practices recorded from these earlier days for pointing the finger at the guilty party, such as watching for a key placed in a book to fall out as the names of suspects were inserted between the pages, or of placing those names, rolled in clay balls, in water to see which would unfold first.

We do still have some methods of drawing lots; there is, of course, the famous "short straw" which we might use to see who is to carry out an honoured task such as making a speech or doing the washing up. This practice has slipped out of the realm of divination, however. Different divination systems grow and decline in importance. Sometimes a breath of life remains in them and may be aroused again to full strength when different social customs or philosophies come into use. Other systems may grow archaic, and be superseded.

Certain divination practices develop over the centuries, especially those with a strong literary or technical basis. Astrology has already been mentioned; there is also the Chinese I Ching, or "Book of Changes". This has been in existence for over three thousand years, and was itself a refinement of earlier forms of oracle divination. Many commentaries have since been added to the I Ching so that the modern classic English edition contains commentaries both by Chinese sages and by the nineteenth-century scholar, Richard Wilhelm. Even the psychologist, C. G. Jung, has something to say in the introductory material. The I Ching, therefore, is a divination system of considerable antiquity, but can be said to have evolved during its existence.

Divination and Magic

There is certainly a difference between divination and magic. Divination does not aim to alter the course of events. This may come about as a consequence, but it is not the purpose of divination. An example of how divination can evolve into a form of active magic comes from Roman times, where a custom for foreseeing good or bad fortune gave rise to an actual attempt to induce beneficial influences. At the Roman New Year, January 1st (the Kalends) was considered to be particularly significant, and everything that happened on that day was seen as a portent of what was to come in the year ahead. To the Romans, this became, therefore, an opportunity to set the year on the right track, by the exchange of presents, later to become our Christmas gift-giving ceremony. In the words of Christina Hole:

> Since [the gifts] were given at New Year, when almost everything was regarded as an omen of good or evil fortune to come, they were often carefully chosen for their luck-bringing properties. Thus, sweets or honey might be given to ensure a year full of sweetness and peace, lamps to fill it with light, and gold, silver, or money to bring prosperity and increasing wealth.
>
> (Christina Hole, *A Dictionary of British Folk Customs*, Hutchinson, 1976)

Here, the celebrants are doing their best to influence the future. Divination does not do this, but plainly this gives rise to ethical problems for its practitioners, since what they say about present or future situations may affect their listeners. More than one astrologer has, in the past, been accused of causing a death by predicting it, and many modern diviners prefer to exercise extreme caution in their pronouncements. A positive benefit of divination is to enhance our sense of purpose and meaning in life, not to reduce it so that we become victims. Some people take a cheerful view of unpleasant predictions, however; in Thailand it is considered a relatively simple matter to avert the fate threatened by inauspicious omens by making religious offerings.

The Limits of Divination

Within this book, I shall not include prophecy – in the sense of Biblical prophets, for instance – or pure clairvoyance. The process of divination involves applying a method which is in some way external to the diviner, such as laying out a pack of cards. Divination involves method and structure, even though these can sometimes be very minimal. The difference between a prophet and a diviner was neatly encapsulated by the sixteenth-century physician and occultist Paracelsus, who said that diviners, astrologers and the like work by "the light of Nature", whereas prophets are directly inspired by the light of God: "I myself avow this, that one prophet in a single hour speaks more certainly and more truly than all the astrologers in many years." This is, perhaps, the distinction between the two rooms described in the image of the castle, one containing fire, the other light.

It could be argued that oracles, such as the one at Delphi, are centres of prophecy, since the priestesses on duty there, sometimes one sole Pythia, at other times two or three, were said to be directly in touch with the divine spirit of Apollo. However, the complicated procedures surrounding the oracle, and the presence of the priests to interpret the ecstatic utterances of the priestesses suggest, at least, that divinatory processes were at work in combination with prophecy. The boundaries between divination, prophecy and clairvoyance are not always easy to draw.

Likewise, the horizon between divination and science is one that changes over the years. Science explains the physical processes at work in the universe; its job is to define the laws of cause and effect as they can be tested at the physical level. Divination makes a leap into the unknown. Its aim is to induce knowledge in ways that are not explicable in physical or natural terms. At least, these are the classic definitions. If a deduction can be shown to arise from the understanding of some natural law, then the process by which it is obtained is not termed divination. In weather lore, both science and divination are used. Predicting a hard winter from a mass of berries on the autumn bushes is based on a theory of natural cycles, assuming that there is a long-term weather pattern with which the layer of plant life is in tune. But sayings such as "If Christmas day on a Sunday fall, A troublesome winter we shall have all", and "If windy on Christmas day, trees will bear much fruit", are purely divinatory, relying on the potent symbolic nature of Christmas Day as a guide to the months ahead. I make no claim that any of these meteorological predictions – scientific or divinatory – work well in practice! But they serve to show how the basis of prediction can be different.

According to the "classic definitions" of science and divination, once a phenomenon can be explained in natural or physical terms, it passes out of the realm of divination into that of science. For instance, of late, evidence has come to light to show that animals and birds may act oddly in the days preceding an earthquake, and scientists would explain this by saying that the creatures are especially sensitive to minute changes in their environment, early-warning signs that a major physical upheaval is about to take place. Animal and bird behaviour could therefore be used as the basis of a scientific prediction of the onset of an earthquake. This is quite different from deducing from the movement of animals or birds that visitors, money or war is coming. Such predictions remain for the time being in the world of divination, since the laws of science cannot possibly assume any causal connection between animal behaviour and these types of events. This illustrates the dividing line commonly drawn between the so-called rational and irrational. But it is not all one-way traffic between the two, with phenomena moving always from the realm of divination to that of science; for science has thrown back into the court of divination and the occult various practices such as astrology and alchemy, having extracted material from them over the years.

These apparently firm definitions may change quite radically in the future, however. At the forefront of science the realization is coming that mind and matter are inseparable, and that consciousness is the source and sustainer of the physical universe. Divination claims to make leaps with the mind into regions where scientific methods cannot penetrate; its vaulting pole, as it were, is the symbolic system that the diviner uses. If scientists become, in some degree, able to accept that consciousness can transcend the boundaries of the individual, and of time and place, then the border between divination and science may come to be seen as a useful boundary, one through which we may freely pass, rather than a kind of Berlin Wall; and, perhaps, a new terminology will be developed which can encompass both disciplines.

Chapter 2

Images of Change

We experience life as a process of change. Our bodies change from youth to old age, our emotions and attitudes are tempered by experience, and we exist in a state of constantly changing activity. Even while asleep, our dreams provide a succession of moving images and we are scarcely still for a moment. Nothing is exempt from change; even rocks are altering under the process of formation and decay. Species evolve, and stars come into being and pass away. Change is movement. When we look for stillness and rest, what we usually experience is rather less movement than usual – a quietening of noise, repose of the body, or relaxation of the mind. The movement of atoms, creatures and planets is often described as a universal dance, which never ceases. As conscious beings, our only way of knowing true stillness is to be unmoved by the movement itself. A skilled dancer may be constantly moving, yet has a repose and balance within that movement.

Finding such repose within our own beings belongs more to the realm of meditation than to divination. However, it is not irrelevant to divination. Usually, divinatory questions are asked because events and situations are experienced as chaotic, hectic movement, or as isolated gestures where no overall "dance" can be perceived. The process of divination involves deciphering the momentum of that movement, seeing where it has come from and where it is going. The structures and language of divination help the diviner to move from a partial, random view of circumstances into the mode where the organisation of life can be perceived to some degree. Knowing change does not stop us being affected by it, but understanding the progress of the dance allows us to move with it gracefully, and even to take a few improvised steps of our own.

Since divination concerns itself with understanding change, it is not surprising that divinatory methods are essentially connected with movement. The flow of movement, the rhythm of cycles, the development of sequence, and points of change provide the fundamental dynamics for operating divination systems. The descriptions of such movements, and their interpretation, then form the language of divination. Let us look first at the categories of movement, the dynamics of divination.

The Process of Divination

Certain divination methods make use of *free-flowing* movement to make their pronouncements. Often these involve the elements earth, water, fire and air. Through the movements of these elements, the diviner gains knowledge. For instance, he may gaze into the rippling surface of water, and allow this to form images, or stare into flames, seeing scenes and pictures that arise there. He may throw a handful of dust into the air and study the cloud that it forms, or scatter earth onto the ground and look at the patterns it makes. These are all methods involving free association of images on behalf of the practitioner, but it is also possible to chart the movements in more specific ways, such as by judging the size, shape, speed or colouring of the forms produced by the movement.

These examples make it clear that the free movement of imagination is also essential to certain divination practices. The borderline separating images without and images within grows very insubstantial here. For instance, gazing into a crystal (traditionally placed in the realm of "water"-based divination) or at one's own thumbnail, both time-honoured methods of divination, generate the flow of images that the diviner needs to give him indications about the matter under investigation. These images may actually be seen within the crystal, or the thumbnail, but they are projections from the imagination. This is a natural ability; we can all see pictures in inkblots, and psychologists have their own way of mapping and assessing this. The diviner, however, stimulates the flow of his imagination in these cases through an external focus, having directed his attention to the question in hand, and with the aim of allowing his imagination to act as a medium through which knowledge may come.

Defined movement is another dynamic used in divination. Here the direction and quality of movement are the chief points noted. For instance, meaning will be assigned to the direction in which a tree trunk falls, in which a bird flies or animals move, and from which lightning appears. As well as natural occurrences, induced movement can also act as a guide in divination. The swing of the dowser's pendulum will show, through the type of movement and its volition, the answer to the question posed.

Arrested movement is equally important. Here, movement is usually created and its halting taken as the point of significance. This halt can be called deliberately; for example, tea-leaves can be swirled around in a cup, then the cup tipped upside down to fix the leaves in a pattern, which is then "read" for meaning. For card-reading, the pack is always shuffled, and this movement ceases at a moment chosen either by the diviner or by the enquirer, with the ordering of the cards then giving the basis for the "lay-out". Movement which ceases of its own accord is also used. One example was given in the last chapter of a divination method involving a key falling out of a book, to find the guilty party, and other methods used included the pointer on a wheel, which comes to rest, or shears in a sieve, which cease to spin. A healthier practice was the old folk custom of opening the family Bible at random, and taking the verse at which the finger came to rest as the one that would rule the family fortunes for the succeeding year.

Occurrences and appearances are yet another way of describing movement. It would probably be better to use the term "change" here, since what we are talking about is single happenings which mark out the unusual from the usual. Within the natural process, something occurs of a different order. Traditionally, these omens have often been celestial eclipses, comets, and dramatic changes in the weather, and in the human world physical signs such as moles, marks, or even pimples appearing on the body, freak births, dreams, unexpected visions, and so on. The meeting of particular birds and beasts on one's path has also been credited with meaning; indeed, the list is endless. These are all omens of change, for which different systems of interpretation have been developed.

Movements which vary from the prescribed sequence can also be the focus of divination. In ceremonial or ritual settings, any unexpected occurrence can be read as highly significant. For instance, it is reported that in the House of Commons in 1601, the Lord Treasurer's secretary fainted in the middle of his speech, generating a heated argument as to whether this was a good or a bad omen! This principle can be extended, in that some rituals are deliberately devised so that every movement or variation can be assessed and often taken as a prediction for the future. Religious animal sacrifices were often conducted in this way, and in traditional Easter games future success in marriage could be judged by seeing how far each person's egg rolled.

Time itself is used as a basis for divination. Time and change, of course, are almost synonymous. Divination practices centred on time usually operate from the view that the passage of time is not uniform, but has moments of heightened potency. For instance, some divination practices are only considered valid if performed at specified key times, such as at New Year, on May Day, or at Hallowe'en. The kinds of questions asked and information received are in keeping with the qualities that these times are considered to embody; the outlook for the year ahead divined at New Year, matters of love and procreation considered at May Day, when the natural energies are waxing, and omens of life and death sought at Hallowe'en, when it is thought that the borders between this world and the next are thin. It is clear that there are different ways of assessing moments of time here, some based on the seasons, and others on religious or social customs.

Divination also makes use of cycles that operate in time, and of making a "snapshot" of a moment in time that reveals the current interplay of these cycles. The classic example is astrology. A horoscope is actually a map of the positions of the planets in the solar system, as seen from a particular point on earth at a particular point in time. Earth and planets revolve around the sun, in cycles of varying lengths, which means that the overall pattern is constantly changing, and that each charting of it reveals a unique picture. A person's horoscope is the celestial chart for the moment of birth. The constancy of planetary cycles, each planet circling against a background of fixed stars, divided into the twelve signs of the zodiac, means that there are fixed principles of interpretation to work from, but the combination of these will be different every time. The different qualities of the planet Mars as it passes through the signs, completing each cycle in about two years, can be assessed, but in each horoscope the planet will appear in a different combination of astrological factors. Astrology is time-based, using planetary cycles as its means of assessing the qualities of moments of time in the past, present and future.

These are the main ways in which we can look at the association between divination, movement and change. It is an essential association, and even in practices where the connection is not always explicit, a little investigation soon reveals this dynamic at work. Divination is an active setting-in-motion; to divine implies that a choice to know has been made, and steps are taken to seek that knowledge.

The Language of Divination

Since the knowledge sought through divination is not coming through the usual channels, it has to be couched in a special language. The senses and the rational faculty may well play a part in divination, but their normal modes of interpreting information are overridden here, since divination seeks the import of a higher order revealing itself through the lesser. The language employed by divination may have its roots in the natural world, but it has to contain more than one level of meaning within it. For instance – to take a banal example – a black cat does not just signify a dark furry creature with four legs and a tail, but "good luck". The language of divination is symbolic, often intensely compressed and capable of many meanings. The diviner's job is to become familiar with the particular vocabulary of any divination system he or she uses, to be aware of the different nuances that it has, and to decide on the particular ones most useful or relevant for the question under consideration.

The time and effort involved in learning a divination language vary enormously, of course; astrology, palmistry and the Tarot can take years to learn, and are often seen as a lifetime's study, whereas a simple "black is no, red is yes" type of language can be summed up in a single sentence. Divination language is based on life principles and has a vocabulary that is comprehensible in terms of human life. The scope of the information that can be given through a particular divination method does depend greatly upon the complexity of the language. There is very little in human life to which astrology cannot be successfully applied; it is a language of extraordinary psychological subtlety but capable also of being related to mundane and material activities. However, both the simple and the complex have their value. A single potent phrase issuing from the Delphic oracle could be enough to alter the fate of nations! All forms of divination language are open to misapplication, although, arguably, the more elaborate structures are less likely to be used casually or mechanically or to produce outright error. It should always be remembered that divination is a combination of the divination system and the diviner, and its success is dependent upon the suitability of the former and the attitude and skill of the latter. We are not examining an area where results are automatic and repeatable; this brings both an exciting challenge and the difficulty of defining how the operation works.

Binary Divination

The simplest form of divination language has a binary structure. Its significators are of a yes/no, neutral/reaction variety. This is divination at its most fundamental, answering enquiries in the affirmative or the negative. An example of this is the basic technique of dowsing. Here the commonly used instruments are a pendulum (small weight or ring suspended on a thread), or a Y-shaped springy stick, or lightweight rods, all of which are held in position without completely restricting the possibility of movement. In traditional water-divining, the Y-shaped stick is grasped by the two ends and held so that the third point stretches ahead of the diviner, parallel to the ground. The "language" of the stick is that the normal carrying position means no reaction, no water, whereas the strong movement downward indicates a positive reaction and the presence of water some way below the surface. The lightweight rods, one in each hand, work on the same principle, except that they swing across one another, horizontally, for a "yes" reading, pointing forward being the neutral, no-reaction signal.

A pendulum operates on a response/no response code, and this response is often further refined so that a "yes" or "no" indication is given by the type of movement made. A movement of the pendulum may indicate the underground presence of water, for instance, while no movement suggests no water; following from this discovery, the dowser may ask: "Is it at five feet . . . ten feet . . .", checking the type of movements to see whether they indicate "yes" or "no". The meaning of the specific movements can vary with individual diviners. A linear swing of the pendulum usually means "yes", and a circular swing "no", but these can be reversed for some people. Aspiring dowsers are usually encouraged to check their own reactions against questions to which the answer is already known, for example by holding the pendulum over an object and asking whether it is their own property, or even by just holding a strong "yes" or "no" in the mind and observing how the pendulum reacts. In practice, a pendulum can be used like a divining rod to dowse for hidden substances, but it is also considered to be a useful instrument for giving answers to particular questions, for indicating healthy or unhealthy areas of the body, or for ascertaining gender. This latter quest has given rise to the popular pastime of trying to determine the sex of an unborn baby by holding a ring suspended on a thread over the expectant mother's stomach. And certain peasant communities in countries such as Thailand claim a high success rate in sexing hen's eggs, the idea being to set the female ones to hatch and eat the male!

Refinements can be added to methods of dowsing, such as using secondary indications to discover how far down the source of water lies, but the basis of the language is binary in its positive-negative framework. Even the apparent trio of neutral/yes/no is really a development of the twofold response, for it begins as a reaction/no reaction system, and then the reaction is further classified into yes or no.

No claims are being made here that dowsing, or any other divination system, is infallibly effective; dowsing is a sensitive operation partly because it is so simple, and it is easy for the diviner to interfere with the process, even though operating with the best of intentions. It is curious, however, that remarkably successful results can sometimes be gained on a first attempt, perhaps because the diviner does not expect too much and is therefore comparatively "innocent". In my own case, some years ago, in a spirit of interested enquiry, I decided to try out map-dowsing. Map-dowsing is a location exercise, where, by operating the yes/no principle, the diviner narrows down the area of enquiry until a precise spot can be pin-pointed. My question was: "Where shall we live next?" At that time we had no immediate thoughts of moving, although it was a possibility for the future. Following the usual procedure, I took a map of the British Isles, divided it in two, and asked whether we would live in side A or side B. The side which elicited the positive response was then bisected, the same question posed and so on. After several similar divisions, the pendulum finally singled out the southern edge of Exmoor as the site of our next house. Deciding that this was a thoroughly unlikely answer – we were living at that time in East Anglia and commuting to London – I put the map and pendulum away and forgot all about my enquiry. However, two years later, we were happily settled in that exact location on the southern side of Exmoor. Only then did I remember this experiment.

It is interesting that the fundamental language of divination should be a binary one, for this is the basis of symmetry and of the development of organic life. A single cell divides and multiplies; the human body is two-sided with its right and left brain, two eyes, ears, arms and legs. Basic systems of number are binary, and our instinctive perceptions are founded on a sense of in front/behind, left/right, black and white, sound and silence. A polarisation of meaning is the first way in which we begin to make sense of the world, as in the infant's sensations of emptiness or fullness, pain or pleasure, light and dark. In a totally unified world we cannot know anything, for there is no comparison. By creating divisions we may begin to discriminate one thing from another, and by multiplying this division build up a whole pattern of recognition. Thus, from a simple polarity or division, complex life forms, languages and perceptions are evolved.

In divination, a binary language can be developed into a more extensive vocabulary. Two popular examples of this are the language of geomancy, and that of the I Ching, the Chinese "Book of Changes", the former relatively straightforward and the latter a subtle and philosophical oracle. Geomancy has been practised in Britain since the Middle Ages, and possibly before. It has been strongly in fashion from time to time and, as it is easy to operate and requires little in the way of equipment, it has provided a pleasant pastime for Victorian ladies and aspiring magicians alike. In theory, it requires a knowledge of astrology, but popular guidebooks to geomancy claimed to do away with that need by providing simplified methods and potted answers. Divination in geomancy consists of building up double and single dots into figures; these figures have names and qualities, and their meaning may be judged individually or by combination.

Each figure is made up of four "rows" of dots and each row consists of either one or two dots. There are sixteen possible figures which can be formed in this way. Thus, out of the basic binary principle, a strong fourfold quality arises; geomancy is said to be an "earth-based" divination, and four is commonly the number ascribed to earth.

Having posed a question, the diviner takes pen and paper and makes four rows of dots, as long or as short as he wishes, but without any conscious thought as to how many dots there should be. He then examines the rows, pairs up the dots and discovers whether the remainder is 0 or 1. For instance, if he has marked seventeen dots, then, since it is an uneven number, a single point will remain, whereas sixteen leaves no remainder. Even rows (no remainder) are then designated by two dots, and uneven rows by a single one. To aid the process of making dots without conscious direction, the diviner may work with closed eyes, or from right to left, in order to free himself from normal patterns of writing. The practice is usually carried out today with pen and paper, but originally marks were made on the earth itself, or on wax tablets, and lengthy preparations were made before the operation could take place, such as purifying a quantity of earth to be used, or calculating favourable celestial times to proceed.

A figure could consist of, for example, a single dot at the top, with three pairs of dots underneath. This particular figure is known as Letitia, and according to one nineteenth-century

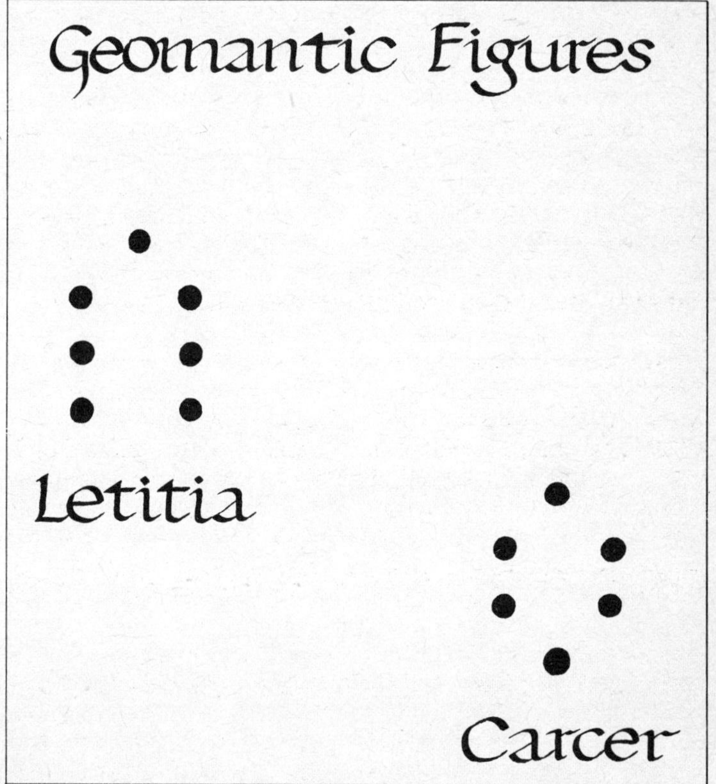

treatise is "the figure emblematical of joy, gladness, fullness of pleasure, and gay delights; endearments, profit, gain, and all favourable things. . . . It is a very fortunate symbol wherever found, and productive of success." On the other hand, if the final pair of dots was replaced by a single one, the figure would be Carcer: this is "the emblem of a prison, imprisonment, close shut-up places, close vessels, and is amazingly evil, as its name imports. It gives loss in all things, poverty and wretchedness, it is also unlucky in every undertaking."

Each figure has an astrological connection, relating to a planet, sign of the zodiac and so on; the import of this becomes clearer when a full geomantic divination takes place. For this, four geomantic figures are arrived at by the method previously described, and then from this a complete set of sixteen is derived. Four figures can give rise to more by using the four top rows to make a new figure, then the four second rows, the third rows and the fourth, increasing the number of figures to eight. Eventually, by more permutations, sixteen figures are arrived at, and these signify the twelve "geomantic houses" (corresponding to the houses of a horoscope), the two "witnesses", the "judge" and a "final result". The houses of a horoscope relate to different areas of life, the first to the individual, the second to possessions, the third to brothers and sisters, etc, and so each geomantic figure is placed in a context which will define its specific interpretation. All the figures have Latin names, such as "Puella", "Caput", and "Acquisitio"; they have strong individual qualities which are then tempered by their position in the reading. The four additional positions in the reading after the twelve houses seem to give an overview of the situation. Thus, from the asking of one question, a complex reading can be made. To do geomancy justice, it would be necessary to have a thorough knowledge of the sixteen figures and an understanding of astrology, but for a simpler version it is possible just to draw up one figure in answer to a question, and to look up its meaning, dispensing with the full setting and the astrological houses altogether.

This gives a brief description of how the language of a binary form of divination is built up, from a very simple odd and even basis into a set of "identities", sixteen forms with distinct characters and titles, which themselves combine in a particular lay-out. It is as if the alphabet of geomancy consists of two letters, whose combinations make sixteen words. These words can be formed into what is almost an infinite variety of sentences; the sentence has an overall significance, and each word will have a different shade of meaning, depending upon its place in the sentence.

To do justice to the I Ching would require an entire volume. Fortunately, there are now books available on this enigmatic and fascinating Chinese oracle, as it has risen from comparative obscurity in the Western world to become a focus of attention and interest. When I bought my own copy of the I Ching, in the late 1960s, I had to apply to the Oriental Department of a specialist bookshop, and was politely asked whether I would like a version in Chinese or English!

The binary language of the I Ching is of broken and straight lines. By methods involving the casting of coins, or the division of a bundle of sticks (traditionally of yarrow), a straight or broken line is indicated, and the process repeated until a figure of six lines is built up, bottom to top, which is known as the hexagram. There are sixty-four hexagrams in all; a single hexagram suffices for a reading as, for each, the Book of Changes gives an "Image", a "Judgement" and many additional commentaries for the enquirer to ponder upon.

The straight lines indicate heaven, the broken earth. Heaven is bright, creative and masculine, while earth is receptive, dark, feminine. A combination of two lines indicates "young" or "old": double broken or double straight lines are "old" and "great", whereas a mixed pair is "young" and "small". Eight triads arise from the fundamental two single lines, the broken and the straight, and these are known as "heaven" (three unbroken lines), "earth" (three broken lines) and "thunder", "wind", "water", "fire", "mountain" and "lake" (the six possible combinations of straight and broken lines). Each of these triads has a wealth of meanings. The primary meanings of "fire", for instance, are warmth, clinging and dependence, and its chief associations are with the middle daughter, the pheasant and the eye. Subsidiary connotations are lightning, helmets, weapons, big-bellied men, the tortoise, the hawk and the crab.

Before moving on to the hexagrams themselves, it is illuminating to point out that here we have a fine example of a divination system with a language founded on basic principles of life, and developed into a vocabulary which encompasses spiritual, psychological, natural and man-made levels of meaning. Every level of meaning has a connection back to those basic principles. This gives the scope for a divination reading to deal with a question originating from any of these levels, or perhaps to give an answer which is not just on that level but which shows the relevance of other levels too. A mundane question may turn out to have spiritual import, and vice versa.

The hexagrams have titles such as "The Well", "Revolution", "The Marrying Maiden" and "Innocence". These meanings are arrived at through the combined influence of the pair of triads that make up each hexagram; it is a complex combination as, within the six lines, further sets of two and of three can be distinguished, and each of the six positions into which a line may fall has its own significance, the fifth line being known as the ruler, for instance. Each line may also be "chang-

I Ching Hexagrams

Fellowship with men

Youthful folly

The arousing

ing"; the original casting of coins or sticks indicates if a broken line is changing to a straight, or the other way round, and each changing line has a particular judgement attached to it.

Thus a potent symbol is reached through the juxtaposition of six lines of two basic types. The symbol gives rise to speculation, as well as to specific hints as to the meaning of the reading; the hexagram is meant to be an exercise in thoughtful contemplation, and tends to reveal the deeper import of a situation rather than give a single prognostication. In many translations the additional commentaries are helpful, as they point out the import of the oracular text and elucidate some of the more enigmatic references, or those which relate to the principles of ancient Chinese society. Unfortunately, there is not space here even to quote a single hexagram in its entirety, but as a partial example here is an extract from hexagram no. 13, "Fellowship with Men", which is composed of the two triads for Heaven and Fire.

The Image
Heaven together with fire
The image of FELLOWSHIP WITH MEN.
Thus the superior man organizes the clans
And makes distinctions between things.

Commentary
Heaven has the same direction of movement as fire, yet it is different from fire. Just as the luminaries in the sky serve for the systematic division and arrangement of time, so human society and all things that really belong together must be organically arranged. Fellowship should not be a mere mingling of individuals or of things – that would be chaos, not fellowship. If fellowship is to lead to order, there must be organization within diversity.

The Lines
Nine at the beginning means:
Fellowship with men at the gate.
No blame.

Commentary
The beginning of union among people should take place before the door. All are equally close to one another. No divergent aims have yet arisen, and one makes no mistakes. The basic principles of any kind of

union must be equally accessible to all concerned. Secret agreements bring misfortune.

(*The I Ching*, Richard Wilhelm translation, Routledge and Kegan Paul, 1951)

Language and Culture

A divination language, therefore, can be demonstrated to be a coherent structure, a self-consistent development of basic principles. If a method of divination at first appears to be absurd or random, it may be a fragmented or popularised version of the original. A child testing her luck by counting magpies – "One for sorrow, two for joy", and so on – is in fact calling upon an ancient and complex tradition which embodies the meaning of number, the search for omens in the natural world, and the attribution of particular significance to birds. Following such a fragment of lore to its source leads to an understanding of how such divination was intended to operate. It is surprising how universal basic methods of divination are; this discovery alone makes the practice worthy of study, for what has held meaning for a large majority of people worldwide over thousands of years has surely something of relevance for human life in general, even in our supposedly cultured and sophisticated age. Divining from the stars, from animals, from the casting of lots and interpretation of symbols are practices common throughout human history.

Any practice of divination will usually have its counterparts in other cultures, although the form and specific vocabulary may differ widely. We have already seen how geomancy in the West and the I Ching from the East have a very similar basis, but expand into highly individual symbols. It would be a mistake to assume that a symbol in one divination system must be identical in meaning to the same symbol used in a different context. But each symbol will have a logical place within its own system, and the foundation of that system will be comprehensible in broad human terms.

An amusing example of cultural differences occurs in the art of divining peaks and troughs of energy in the landscape. In the

Chinese tradition of geomancy, "Feng-Shui", great attention is paid to discovering the most potent and beneficial sites upon which to build, using techniques to locate the "dragon lines" of energy passing through the earth. Such lines are never straight; it is said that straight lines can destroy the power of the dragon: "Generally speaking, all straight lines are evil indications, but most especially when a straight line points directly towards the spot where a hsueh (dragon lair) has been chosen." (Stephen Skinner, *The Living Earth Manual of Feng-Shui*, Routledge and Kegan Paul, 1982). Straight lines, known as "hidden arrows", include not only natural rock formations but also lines of rooftops, railway lines or even television aerials. A contrast to the Chinese definition of power comes in the currently popular Western practice of searching for "ley lines" linking ancient megaliths, barrows and so on. These lines are thought to channel powerful currents of energy, and they are always straight. Both the Chinese and the Western systems have their roots in divining the inherent qualities of the earth and its landscape, but plainly the language of the two systems is different and not directly interchangeable. If a full study were to be made of each practice it could most probably be discovered, from the internal logic and symbolism of each, how this divergence arose. It may well be, for instance, that the Chinese are intent on searching out innate natural patterns of energy, and consider anything "unnatural" or artificial – such as straight lines – to be antipathetic to that; whereas ley lines may have their origin in human endeavour to create a network of energy and communication over the countryside, finding straight lines to be the most efficient and effective way of doing it.

This underlines the fact that a divination language must be learnt in its entirety. Such a language has its own grammar and vocabulary, and a meaningful language cannot be constructed by tacking together bits of several different languages. In the days of the eminent Victorian scholar, Sir James Frazer, whose magical and folkloristic gleanings filled several volumes known as *The Golden Bough*, researchers tended to assume that universal meanings could be attributed to symbols and practices. Later, a reaction against this postulated that a universal significance was lacking, and that even within a single symbolic system one symbol was just as effective as another. Such an argument is described by Keith Thomas in *Religion and the Decline of Magic* (1971), a volume containing much interesting material but written with the aim of dismissing divination and symbolically-based practices as degenerate forms of superstition. He suggests that:

> These systems may involve postulating symbolic analogies between human beings and plants, animals or birds and other parts of natural creation. . . . The symbols themselves are arbitrarily chosen. They have no meaning, save that given by their position within the code.

The suggestion that symbols have a particular significance within their own context is surely sensible, but to call the choosing of those symbols random seems a sweeping and superficial judgement.

Types of Language

Let us now look more closely at some of the areas from which divination systems derive their vocabularies. These can be divided into four broad categories: natural, celestial, human and symbolic. Many divination practices have affinities with more than one category; the aim of this classification is not to sum up every method of divination, but to show how man has drawn the language for it from the world around him, from the world of space and stars and from human experience, and how he has constructed symbols from numbers and images.

THE NATURAL WORLD

The kingdom of nature provides plentiful material for a language of divination. To make sense of practices where changes in the weather and in the behaviour of birds and beasts are related to future events in human life, a different outlook is needed. If we are concerned only with our personal identity, we may view the reading of importance into external phenomena as a primitive way of projecting our personal ideas onto the external world. But if we are able to conceive that our individual identity is a small part of a greater identity, like a cell within a body, then the possibilities extend just as our world extends.

Within that greater sphere, a greater extent of knowledge is available; man can choose to seek it out there.

It is commonly acknowledged that man is a creative being; he is not fixed to one pattern of behaviour, but has the ability to shape and extend his world. Thus a person may decide: "I am going to extend my world to include that of the animals around me." If we have within us, as the Renaissance philosophers said, all the qualities of other forms of life, such as animals, plants and minerals, then, in theory, it is possible to extend our attention to include another chosen level of creation. There are resonances existing between human and natural life and, indeed, those same philosophers emphasised, between the human, celestial and angelic worlds, too. All this suggests that identity is in some manner a matter of choice; we can keep it small, as personal survival dictates for much of the time, or we can allow it to include more, to broaden the field of knowledge open to us.

This image of extending the sphere of experience is actually formulated in certain divination practices.

In divining through the movements of animals and birds, a sphere – or at any rate a circle – is described by the terms of the operation. In the classical system of watching bird activities for omens, for instance, the area under observation is called "the templum" and the bird's flight interpreted in relation to the position of the observer. A bird passing by and coming to rest on the left is evil, whereas one resting on the right is fortunate. A bird moving across one's path and flying away out of sight from left to right is good, and from right to left evil. Straight and curving lines of flight, behind and ahead, to left and right, all build up a spatial picture in which the observer and the bird form what is in effect a hemisphere, and their mutual positioning is the code to be interpreted. Within this unit, the relative merits of left and right are heavily stressed, according to the traditional Roman designation of "dextra", or right, as good, and "sinistra" or left, as bad – the old binary basis once more.

We may find such a practice amusingly naive. Personally, I do not think that such a divination system would be effective unless a great deal of attention was customarily paid to one's own relation to birds in flight and at rest, and an awareness of this sphere of interaction was built up. The instructions given by

Agrippa in the Renaissance are to notice the birds "when thou shalt go out of thy house to do any business"; in a spirit of curious enquiry I once decided to follow this procedure and see if I could bring the system to life. After I had left the house on about ten occasions and failed even to remember to look for birds, I came to the conclusion that these practices are at the very least excellent forms of training the memory and the attention! And attention is itself a key factor in any practice of divination.

The idea of a sphere of operation is linked to that of the wholeness which a divination system must have. As I have already pointed out, a divination practice which is apparently fragmentary, or simply an assortment of instructions, usually originates from a much more unified system. Even a well-formulated system, with a coherent language, may itself relate to a greater living unity. To make this clearer, let us take the example of divination through listening to the cries of birds. Here the type of cry and the place from which it is heard give rise to divinatory interpretations. An extensive example of ancient lore relating to raven cries is given in *Pagan Celtic Britain*, by Anne Ross (Routledge and Kegan Paul, 1967), from which the following extracts are taken:

> If the raven call from above an enclosed bed in the midst of the house, it is a distinguished grey-haired guest or clerics that are coming to you, but there is a difference between them. If it be a lay cleric the raven says "bacach"; if it be a man in orders it says "gradh gradh" and twice in the day it calls. If it be warrior guests or satirists that are coming, it is "gracc gracc" it calls, or "grob grob", and it calls in the quarter behind you, and it is from there the guests are coming. . . . If women are coming it calls long. If it calls from the northeast end of the house, robbers are about to steal the horses . . .

This is a very elaborate language, the above quotation being only a fraction of the complete teaching. But it seems that even this complex system is only a partial revelation of a greater ability, that of understanding completely the language of birds. As Anne Ross points out:

> Not only were the cries of ravens believed to be capable of interpretation by Druids and other trained people, but certain people were

popularly believed to have the 'language of birds' and to be capable of understanding the speech of ravens and of holding conversation with them. There are numerous examples of this belief in the traditions of the Celtic world, and it is also found widely in other culture groups.

We have here a suggestion that man can direct his consciousness so that it is in tune with the consciousness of birds, and can learn from them. Such a gift takes us, I think, out of the realm of divination proper, and into that of prophecy and shamanism, for it is not quite the application of a method to venture into the unknown, but a direct process of knowing. This is the same distinction as I have already drawn between the prophet and the diviner. Such complete attunement to the world of nature is known both in the practice of shamanism and nearer to home, where we have the famous example of St Francis and his powers of communicating with animals and birds.

Using a divinatory system can often be a safer path, for it is easy to be overwhelmed by fantasy when there is no disciplined structure to apply. It may be very difficult to live a normal, everyday life *and* to be attuned to the world of other living creatures. Our individual identity, which to some extent must dissolve in order to gain access to this more expansive order of consciousness, is necessary to give us limits and protect us from energies too powerful to handle. Divination gives us a means of learning about the unknown without releasing the security of the known; we may feel in a different state of awareness, but divination rarely involves trance or total loss of self-control.

However, a warning note should be sounded here. A false kind of divination, or attunement to the world around, is found in certain cases of mental illness and instability – for instance, in paranoia and obsession. Here, the person may believe that every line in the pavement is a coded language, which, if he could decipher it, would reveal the true identity of his persecutors, be a message from a lost love, or tell him, indeed, the great secrets of the universe. I am no expert in the field of psychology, but it does seem possible that many of those afflicted with severe mental problems may indeed be sensitive to psychic influences, to the presence and significance of the world around them, but lack the discrimination and stability to deal with it. Thus personal fears and wishes are easily projected into such powerful impressions.

Another situation to be wary of is one in which you are falsely tempted to read a nucleus of connected events or images as indications of future events. The psychologist C. G. Jung notes that very often the "outside" world seems to echo inner developments in the individual; this can be treated as a statement more of what is going on, than of what is to come. This principle is often termed "synchronicity". For instance, he developed a powerful inner image of a figure called "Philemon", who had the wings of a kingfisher; soon after, he found a dead kingfisher in his garden. I, too, can recall such a sequence: in one day I saw a kingfisher flying down the river in our village (a rare occurrence), came across an insect with the brilliant hues of a kingfisher, and heard a member of the group I was teaching report that she could see a very strong image of a kingfisher in her mind. I did not try hard to find out the "meaning" of all this, but it is likely that it was an indication of the stage the group had reached, and that, as its leader, I would be particularly attuned to "picking up" signs of this. Such clusters of occurrences, often spanning the worlds of dreams, imagination and "reality", are surely known to most of us; they can give us useful confirmation or insights into current situations but should not necessarily be treated as omens of the future.

Returning to the theme of a divination language founded on natural phenomena, it should be said that there are many others apart from those based on the flight and cries of birds. Other languages derived from the natural world may relate to the weather, to the appearance of plants and animals, to cloud formations, to the croaking of frogs, the sounding of thunder, the rise and fall of water and, indeed, to anything of a natural or elemental order. Fragments of these divinatory systems have passed into latter-day folklore and into the practices of children, who are often the final guardians of dying magical practices. "A black beetle crawling on your shoe means that one of your friends is going to die", "If a bird dirts on you it is lucky", "If you see a flock of birds you must cross your legs and wish", "To see a white cat on the way to school is taken to be a sign of trouble ahead" and "If a rabbit crosses your path in front it is lucky but if it passes by the back it is unlucky" are just some of the examples given by Iona and Peter Opie in *The Lore and Language of Schoolchildren* (Oxford University Press, 1959).

THE CELESTIAL WORLD

The chief practice of divining through celestial phenomena is astrology. We have already looked at this briefly, in connection with ideas of time in divination, but will examine it in greater depth here, in terms of its language and symbolism. Astrology is flourishing today; it has evolved over the centuries and its language has proved capable of expressing subtle psychological insights in accordance with a twentieth-century approach as well as giving material predictions and assessments of national and political situations. The major form of astrology in use at present is natal astrology, which divines the character, potential and life development of an individual from the pattern of the solar system as it was at the moment of birth. The form of astrology most commonly classed as divinatory is horary ("of the hour") astrology, in which a specific question is posed, a chart drawn up for the moment of asking the question, and the answer judged from the tenor of the chart. But it is hard to see why natal astrology, looked at objectively, should not be classed as a form of divination too. Certainly natal and horary astrology share the same celestial vocabulary, applied with slightly different rules. Horary, perhaps, is a more obvious case of venturing into the unknown, using a technique which is most definitely beyond the usual understanding of cause and effect. Some natal astrologers prefer to think of their study as a science which will, eventually, be provable by normal scientific tests, and it is true that natal astrology today has gained much of its strength and credibility through absorbing psychological models of interpretation, whereas horary is a purely symbolic form of astrology. But all forms of astrology are based on the assumption that life on earth and the patterns of planets and stars in the sky are vitally connected.

From watching the patterns of natural phenomena on earth, we turn, with astrology, to interpreting those of the solar system, the next "unit" or sphere of identity up the scale. Through "reading" the heavens, taking the positions of the sun, moon and planets as they relate to each other and to the background of fixed stars, astrologers can describe the qualities that correspond with the particular moment in time for which the reading is taken, and relate them to human life. A celestial "snapshot" is taken, its features interpreted through the language of astrology, and the interpretation applied to whatever is born of that moment on earth, whether it is an event or a person. In fact, the picture will vary, depending upon the place on earth chosen, giving, for instance, a somewhat different astrological reading for a child born in London than for a child born in New York at the same moment. The "snapshot" is not, of course, a literal photograph, but a stylised map drawn up to show the planets and their relationship to the local horizon; it is this map which is known as the "horoscope".

The planets are the key feature of any horoscope, the term "planets" in astrology including the sun and moon. Basically, the planets are viewed as the principles of creation. They have been seen as gods, as ministers of divine will, as universal archetypes and as vital forces operating in the human psyche. As in any strong symbolic system, they lend themselves to various forms of description. Until comparatively recently, only seven "planets" were known. The two "Lights" were the Sun, recognised as the principle of life, vitality and individuality, and the Moon, recognised as dependence, imagination and mutability. Of the faster-moving planets, Mercury signified communication, intelligence and agility, Venus beauty, pleasure and sensuality, and Mars vigour, aggression and ambition. The two slower-moving planets were Jupiter – joviality, loyalty, fruitfulness, and Saturn – limitation, commitment and understanding. All these meanings remain, but as the three outer planets, Uranus, Neptune and Pluto, were discovered, so meanings for them were also evolved and the extra trio were incorporated into the astrological pantheon. Uranus represents change, originality and inspiration, Neptune mysticism, dissolution and transcendence, and Pluto death, rebirth and potency.

Many more terms could be added to these, because the planets represent principles which can be applied to any level of life. While Jupiter represents ceremonial forms of religion, at the other end of the spectrum the horse is also assigned to

Jupiter, being rather large and noble in bearing! The astrological language is capable of almost infinite shaping and formulation, while remaining true to its founding principles. There is no hard-and-fast list of all attributes of and associations with the planets; the insight and common sense of the astrologer must determine what is an effective interpretation in each case.

Although the popular belief is often that the zodiac signs are the chief elements in astrology, they are really a secondary feature, in that they give colouring to the planets in the context of the horoscope. The term "zodiac" means "circle of animals". The zodiac is the plane of the solar system extended into space. The solar system is almost flat, as though the sun, moon and planets are laid out on an invisible plate. If the rim of this plate were drawn around the sky, it would represent the pathway along which the planets move, and by dividing this great circle, or "ecliptic", into twelve equal sections, we arrive at the twelve signs of the zodiac. Each division is given a symbol such as Cancer (The Crab), Leo (The Lion) and Capricorn (The Goat) and these emblems, chiefly of beasts, give rise to the collective title. Each sign can be described as a mode of being, as a psychological typecasting. A planet is then characterised and defined according to the sign it is in at the time of drawing up the horoscope. For instance, Mercury in Libra will give a person pleasant speech and manners but an indecisive attitude in mental work, since Mercury rules communication and the mind, and Libra, the sign of the balance, represents a way of operating that likes to please and to weigh up alternatives. What we think of as our sign is in fact the position of the sun in the zodiac at the time of birth.

The language of astrology is indeed a complex one and usually takes several years to master. Not only are there planets and signs in a chart, but also "houses", a further set of twelve divisions which are reckoned as departments of life – the fourth representing the home, the seventh marriage, for instance. In addition, the planets make aspects between each other – angular relationships based on the number of degrees apart that one planet lies from another in the zodiacal circle. The language of a complete horoscope, therefore, involves judging the planets according to the signs and houses in which they lie, and the connections between them. It can be said that the planets are the dramatis personae, the signs their costumes, and the houses the stage sets that they use.

Astrology is the queen of celestial arts, but before leaving that category it is worth mentioning that other groups of phenomena have been studied in connection with the heavens. Comets, eclipses and lunar phases have all been used for divinatory purposes, both on their own and in conjunction with astrology. It should also be pointed out that the astrology I have just described is a Western form, and that Indian, Chinese and South American Indian astrology differ to a greater or lesser degree from the astrology with which we are familiar. Divination methods may use the same framework, but employ a different language to describe it.

THE HUMAN SPHERE

Phenomena of human physique and consciousness give rise to many branches of divination. It is a long-held assumption that our character and future life can be read from our external appearance; the problem then is to decide what the language of the body is saying. Some people seem to have a natural gift for this, as was the case with Lady Lucy Hester Stanhope (1776–1839), an intrepid traveller and eccentric. Her faithful friend and physician recorded: "She had a remarkable talent for divining characters by the conformation of men . . . it was after she went to live in solitude that her penetration became so extraordinary." Her own explanation of this skill was that she would read people's faces just as a gardener looking at twenty flowers can tell you about their type, growth patterns, and how long they will live.

Other approaches are far more precise, and lend themselves more readily to being taught. Specific techniques of face-reading concentrate on the shape of the features, distance apart of eyes and brows, colour of hair and eyes, bone structure, and so on. In *Arcandam Peritissimus*, a sixteenth-century treatise on astrology and divination, the art of eyebrow-reading is accorded a special place: "The eyebrows large show the man to be arrogant, and without shame . . . the eyebrows which descend crooked on the side of the nose declare the man to be witty in naughty things." Divinatory face-reading claims a very intimate connection between psyche and physiognomy, going further than the usual assumption that we can tell something about a person's character by the lines on the face, the set of the jaw, and so on.

In the nineteenth century there was a fashion for practising phrenology, judging temperament and ability by the bumps on the skull. Different areas of the skull were held to relate to particular aspects of human nature, and the interested student could join a special phrenological society, attend lectures and even sit diploma examinations in his chosen subject. Phrenology is not, at the present time of writing, a survivor in the divinatory field. When a divination system claims to be thoroughly scientific it soon loses credibility. Divination proper does not stand up to conventional scientific testing, even though there may be overlapping areas with science and certainly with psychology.

Divination will often build a language from changeable phenomena, for these can be allied to changeability of life, and be interpreted as forerunners of particular events and conditions. Hence the appearance of moles, marks and even pimples has provoked much interest, the art of "pimple divining" having been developed into an elaborate and rather amusing art in Thailand. Black or vermillion pimples are considered most fortunate, but red, white or yellow ones unlucky. Groups of seven or five pimples are the best numbers to have, indicating wealth if they appear on the left side and promotion on the right. Sometimes it seems that the more uncomfortable the blemish, the happier the prognostication: "A pimple on the eyeball means that person will be grateful to parents." Even specific formations may be identified: "If a group of seven are arranged on the forehead in the W-shape of the constellation Cassiopeia, this is most lucky." (H. G. Quaritch Wales, *Divination in Thailand*, Curzon Press, 1983).

Palmistry, which is the reading of life and character from lines on the hands, allows for flexibility of our fortunes, since these lines can and do change over the years. The lines on the left hand are commonly interpreted as signifying the nature with which one is born, and those on the right hand what one has made of it. The full language of palmistry is a complex one,

The Palm of the Hand

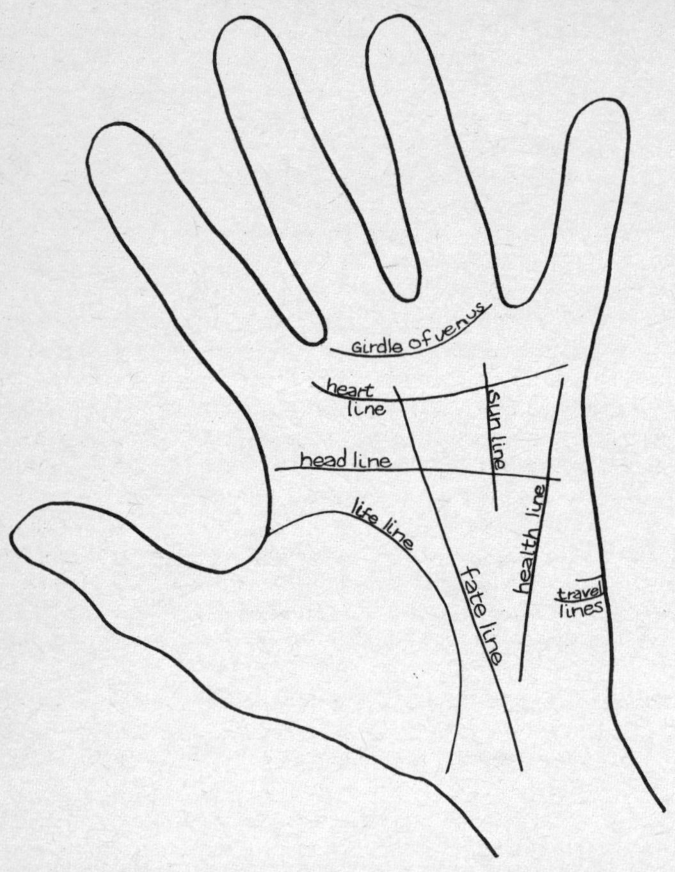

for it includes the meaning of lines on different parts of the palm, specifically interpreted by their length, strength and so on, plus the shape of fingers, palm, joints, fleshy mounds and the condition of the nails and skin. We see the idea of time closely bound into its symbolism, since a line on the hand representing time means that developments in the past and future can be judged by reading along that line. Thus palmistry contains the interesting and valuable notion that we can change our futures, for, if the future can be read from the lines, but the lines themselves can change, then clearly we have an option to take charge of our future. Palmistry does not tell us how to do this, but implies that it is possible. The language of palmistry shows how the grammar and vocabulary of a divination language actually make a statement about the nature of human beings, and human potential. Divination, effectively applied, is a freeing not a restricting process.

The phenomena of human consciousness which lend themselves most readily to the divinatory process are dreams. Dreams were called "the oldest oracle" by Plutarch. The language here is most fluid, for there are no limits to the images that may occur in dreams. It seems to be accepted among people of all ages and races that dreams can reveal the future, or bring to light facts about the present or past which were previously unknown. It also seems to be understood that dreams may be of different orders – some arising from physical conditions, others stemming from current preoccupations, and only certain ones true revelations in the divinatory sense. The ancient Greeks held the view that the soul could show its real nature when the body slept, and was free to draw to itself knowledge of another order that the waking mind could not grasp.

They also practised the art of inducing dreams which would act as guiding visions in curing illness or problems. This technique, of encouraging dreams which could be divined for meaning, was not unique to the classical age. The initiation ordeal of American Indian shamans may include imprisonment in a dark pit for several days, the aim being to invoke a definitive dream or vision which will determine the new shaman's special gifts and missions. Closer to home, the Renaissance magus Cornelius Agrippa states: "Whosoever would receive divine dreams, let him be well disposed in his body, his brain free from vapours, and his mind from perturbations, and let him that day abstain from supper, neither let him drink that which will inebriate, let him have a clean and neat chamber, also exorcized and consecrated: in the which, a perfume being made, his temples anointed, things causing dreams being put on his fingers, and the representation of the heavens being put under his head, and paper being consecrated, his prayers being said, let him go to bed, earnestly meditating on that thing he desireth to know.: So he shall see most true and certain dreams with the true illumination of his intellect." The poet W. B. Yeats, a keen experimenter in magical practice, used to put certain kinds of plants or symbols under his pillow at night in the hope of inducing dreams of a related order. His method of using "correspondences" would involve choosing an appropriate object, such as a herb, symbolic device, and so on, ruled by a particular planet, in order to invoke a dream of that planetary quality.

Different cultures have also suggested that there are special times for having dreams which lend themselves to divinatory interpretation. Agrippa mentions the "Matutine" dreams, experienced between sleeping and waking, as being most potent, and in the Buddhist tradition dreaming is divided into three stages, according to the three parts of the night. The first stage produces dreams which are connected with bodily functions and digestion, in the second stage dreams derive from the mental processing of the day's impressions and experiences, while during the third stage dreams are said to come from the Gods, and may carry revelations of great importance.

There are plenty of guides on the market to working out what one's dreams portend, for most of us like to know what our dreams mean. However, lists of specific meanings are never going to be entirely successful, for factors of personal association and cultural conditioning will colour dreams strongly. The language of dream books has its own logic, and strikes a few psychological truths, but the books are likely to be read more as an amusing pastime than for insight. There is frequent use of the idea of reversal as a guide to meaning – that death, for instance, means a birth, and that to dream of a honeymoon indicates disappointments. This is an interesting concept, perhaps implying that dream life is a mirror image of our waking one. Other interpretations may be based on direct association, so that to dream of a Humming Bird, for instance, means "travel to a foreign clime and successful business there" (*The Mystic*

Dream Book, Foulsham). The association of going abroad, to an exotic place such as where the humming bird lives, is easily understood, and perhaps the mention of successful business is allied with the humming bird's ability to extract nectar from a flower.

One would not expect such symbols to have universal significance in guides to dream interpretation, although there are correlations: in Thailand, to dream of riding an elephant shows that wealth is coming, and in the British popular dream language the elephant is also thought of as helpful, showing that assistance will come from outside sources. But when our guide (*The Mystic Dream Book*) advises us that a dream of a horse can only be judged by reference to its colour, surely we are once more back in the business of deriving omens from magic and myth. From psychological associations we move to the realm where the gods and man walk together, where white horses are supernatural and sacred, and black dogs an omen of sudden death. What in general passes for a language of dream interpretation may in fact be a mixture of attributes from different systems, and it may be that in the West we lack a clear divinatory language of dreams, although we have developed a splendid psychological understanding of their import.

No psychologist worth his salt will use a fixed list of meanings when interpreting the dreams of patients, and diviners of dreams might be well advised to follow this example. This, of course, is a highly difficult task. The division which usually exists between looking at dreams as precognitive states and as psychological revelations is unsatisfactory, although certain experts on dreams are beginning to bridge that gap. (See Lyn Webster's *Dream-work: guide to the midnight city*, Dryad Press, 1987). For the moment, the diviner of dreams may have to rely a great deal on his intuition and insight into the nature of the dreamer. A Sufi teacher in Turkey once illustrated to me the problem of dealing with dreams that may on the surface appear similar but stem from quite different causes and give rise to different prognostications. He related how, within a short space of time, he was visited by two men, both claiming to have dreamed of climbing up the minaret of a mosque and of giving the call to prayer. To the first, he revealed that he had stolen some goods, that the theft would shortly come to light, and that he would be publicly disgraced. To the second, he indicated that he would soon have an opportunity to make a much desired pilgrimage to Mecca. The interpretation of both dreams proved accurate.

PATTERNS, NUMBERS AND SYMBOLS

Our last category in this survey of divination language is that of systems constructed solely on number, geometry or symbol. People have always been interested in discerning the innate properties of number. An example of interpretation is that one indicates a unified, integrated whole, whereas two becomes a polarity, the formation of masculine and feminine, and three the dynamic but self-contained triad. The classical school of Pythagorean philosophers set great store by the power of number, although we do not, unfortunately, have detailed knowledge of their methods. The Hebrews associate each letter of their alphabet with a number; thus each word and every sentence have a numerical value. By various permutations of letters and numbers different orderings and meanings can be gleaned – a divinatory practice known as "Gematria" which is often used to discover assumed hidden revelations in the scriptures.

Such an interplay of numbers and letters may be used in divination through numerology, where, for instance, a person's name becomes a number by equating each letter with a figure, adding these figures together, and reducing the result down to a single digit by further addition, in the way that 18 becomes 9 when the two figures are added. In more complicated practices, dates and times may be added to names, and more elaborate calculations carried out until, from the final numberings, a judgement can be made on the nature of the person or the likely outcome of the enterprise. Although this can turn into both a mechanical and obsessive occupation, undoubtedly divination through number has its origins in a serious appreciation of the properties of number, an attempt to perceive the essence of a situation by equating it with number. Growth in the natural world is indeed bound up with number, for plant and crystal forms are all based on numerical principles, and underlying the multiplicity of growth simpler, numerical structures can be perceived.

While numerology may appeal to those who enjoy the abstract, divination through symbols is the province of those who like to work with the imagination, but who prefer the language used to be more precisely defined than is the case in the completely free-form practices mentioned earlier. The ordinary pack of playing cards has a language which combines both numbers and symbols; its numbering must be interpreted according to the meaning of the individual numbers, while its pictorial cards and its suits are symbolic emblems. In a lay-out, the Queen of Spades may represent a dark lady, the suit of hearts love and joy, and that of clubs anger and struggle, for instance. In recent years the practice of "reading the Runes" has been revived, in which ancient Norse letter-signs are used in their symbolic forms, taking on images such as "the wild ox", "the torch", and "the yew tree". It is uncertain whether the modern practice has much in common with the original rune divination, but that in itself is no obstacle to its providing a successful divinatory language to work with.

In order to give the use of symbols in divination the space that it deserves, I am devoting the whole of the next chapter to a description and discussion of the Tarot pack. This is the most evocative and vivid set of symbols that we have available to us as a divinatory method. To open the present chapter, I set out the idea that movement and change provide the motivation for divination, then showed how number, stemming from a simple two-fold division, creates its structure. Finally we reach the stage where the imagination is brought into play, through the contemplation of the symbolic language in which divinatory knowledge may be embodied.

Chapter 3

The Tarot – The Symbolic Circus

In this chapter, I take the opportunity to look at one particular divination system in depth – the Tarot. This is a set of pictorial cards, each with a different emblem and title. As it is a relatively compact system, I shall be able to discuss each of its symbols, set them in a historical context, and indicate how they might be interpreted in a reading. It will be necessary to restrict the scope to the Major Arcana (see below), and to giving a general guide to the cards, rather than describing methods for carrying out readings. The Tarot is a fascinating collection of images which can be studied fruitfully in their own right, and I hope to give some clues as to how this may be done; for readers wishing to take work with the Tarot further, there are many practical books available to help.

The Common Life of Symbols

What is the Tarot? In modern Western society it has a colourful reputation – mysterious, dangerous, powerful, magical. It is associated in the popular imagination with psychic trances, with fortune-telling gypsies and pagan practices. Superstition has gathered around it, and those who have dealings with the Tarot have been credited with undue influence over their fellow human beings. Much of this is myth, upheld by those who have probably never even held a Tarot pack and looked through the cards it contains. A divination system is, after all, created by man; it is a human mode of expression, a language devised to bridge the gap between the known and the unknown.

But it would be foolish to dismiss completely the mystique that has built up around the cards. Their history is curiously hard to pin down, as we shall see; their origins and the means of their propagation are unknown, and yet they turn up in many different countries and at all levels of society. It is almost as if they have a life of their own. I say *almost* as if, because I think it is this that lies at the root of popular wariness of the cards. It is when we feel that objects or symbols *do* have a life of their own that we are most likely to react irrationally, from an instinctive fear that we shall be controlled, rather than control. I would suggest, however, that the Tarot has established itself within the collective psyche of the Western world, and it is this greater source of life that we may be perceiving when we start to study the cards.

If the premise is accepted that there is a greater human consciousness in operation beyond that of the individual, then it is possible that within this "mind of man" – or even within a localised area of the "mind" pertaining to a particular culture or period in history – ideas and forms of knowledge can take hold, grow, and be productive, just as they can within an individual's personal sphere of consciousness. The idea of a greater human consciousness, often credited to the psychologist C. G. Jung, under the title of "the collective unconscious", is in fact a much older and more universally accepted concept, but has been made understandable in modern terms by the work of Jung. It also promises to be brought even more up to date by the work of Rupert Sheldrake, a scientist whose theory of "morphic resonance" suggests that the learning process is not restricted to individual experience but covers a broader spectrum of consciousness. According to this theory, if a person or even an animal faces a new puzzle or challenge, and masters it, the next person or creature to be confronted with the same problem, even if there is no direct connection whatsoever with the original mind that tackled it, will reach a solution more quickly. This is the general basis for Sheldrake's work, which obviously in practice needs far more complex interpretation and determination.

If we have access to a more generalised area of mind, then we may also be able to tap the images and forms of thought that lie there. Just what such images and forms are, of course, is a huge question. But they may emerge in the myths, symbols and systems of knowledge that we have created, shaping the raw archetypal material of the collective mind into specific forms that still carry the potent charge of the supra-personal. If such a creation carries the life of the collective consciousness within it, and yet is comprehensible to the ordinary mind too, then it is a powerful medium. Moreover, it will seem to have its own volition; it will be capable of being adapted to other times and other ways of thought, of serving different purposes, and of appearing in differing types of images. It draws its sustenance from a common truth, yet can be manifested in ways which accord with specific needs.

In case this seems too abstract, two other examples apart from the Tarot may help to clarify the point. The first is folk song, and the second alchemy. The history of both is mysterious and we do not know exactly how they evolved. Elements of British folk song can be traced to the ancient Middle East, and even further afield geographically, while alchemy flowers, dies down and flowers again, from classical times onwards. By folk song are meant the songs which were mainly handed down by "oral tradition", and which turn up in different versions in different times and places, changed in detail and colour, but similar in essence. Sometimes such songs were written down, made more literary, or "gentrified" for the drawing room, but always the life of the folk song re-establishes itself, throwing off a poetic gloss or fashionable musical embellishments as these lose their appeal, often becoming more simple and mythical again until a new generation has another bright idea about how to dress up folk music. Folk music weaves itself in and out of popular culture, peasant culture, "classical" music, political comment, low comedy, refined poetry, and adapts to almost any other influence one cares to mention. We can say that folk music seems "almost to have a life of its own" as we can say the same about the Tarot. In the case of folk music, we don't find that "life" threatening today, but there have certainly been times in history when this has been so, and the singing of folk songs has been banned as dangerous to politics, to the Church, or to honest toil.

So, forms of knowledge and of art which spring up from the collective mind possess a vitality and volition which may be mistaken for an "anti-human" force. Alchemy, too, has such a vitality and has also been considered powerful and dangerous at different periods of its lengthy history. The alchemist was considered mad, obsessed, and sometimes even in league with the devil. Satirists of the eighteenth century and earlier often depicted the alchemist as the man in the grip of a fanatical passion, eyes burning, clothes ragged and filthy in appearance, while his wife and children beseech him in vain for money to buy food. The popular understanding of alchemy was that it was the quest to make gold out of base material, and, put like this, it certainly seems to appeal to the most greedy and obsessive instincts in man. However, the true alchemical search was as much about spiritual perfection as about practical miracles, and many alchemical writers were at pains to point out that the gold they strove after was not the common metal but an elixir of life, or "the Philosophers' Stone". It seems that the practice of alchemy was a mixture of spiritual striving and chemical experiment. Indeed, the two were considered related, there being no firm division between the being of the alchemist and the chemical reactions in the vessel which he tended over the fire.

This extraordinary process was usually represented through enigmatic texts and striking symbols, in which "green dragon", "black raven" and "the marriage of the King and Queen", for example, could represent stages of personal growth as well as changes in substance. True to the kind of tradition I am describing, rooted in archetype, the forms of these images could vary widely, and no treatises on alchemy were ever the same. But they derive, recognisably, from the same source. All the images are concerned with the process of transformation, and are thus shaped around such motifs as the changing of one colour into another, of warring animals which devour each other, of death and rebirth, and of the enclosing crystal or vessel in which these changes must be provoked and observed. There is a language of alchemical imagery, varied in its application and combination of words, but distinct and recognisable to anyone who has once come into contact with it.

Now, it also seems that a symbolic language, once created, can be absorbed back into the collective psyche again, in the same way that an individual mind retains impressions. This model of human consciousness suggests a collective mind that is active, evolving and retentive, from which we can draw and into which our creations flow when we have given them form. The more powerful and relevant the images we shape, the more likely they are to influence the human psyche; such a suggestion implies that our creativity carries great potential power, and hence great responsibility. Such an ability of image and myth to change the existing viewpoint was recognised and feared by the ancients; the chief accusation against the Greek philosopher Socrates, and which condemned him to die, was that he had introduced new deities into the city of Athens. However, while this idea of the far-reaching effects of human consciousness is certainly not irrelevant to divination, it is peripheral to the point about alchemy.

Alchemy built up a variable but recognisable language of imagery, and this language appears to have remained, to a certain extent at least, within the psyche of man. C. G. Jung found to his astonishment that in his own dreams and in those of some of his patients, alchemical images were occurring of which they had no previous conscious knowledge. The person concerned had not come across such images in books, paintings and so on, but had produced them "spontaneously" from the "unconscious". The author has had similar experiences; one dream in particular, occurring around the age of twenty, was full of charged, potent images, terrifying in their intensity, which I only came to recognise afterwards as arising directly from an alchemical/cabbalistic tradition. In my own case, the dream marked a turning point in my life. In the case of Jung's patients, he also found that such symbols were pointers to changes occurring in their being, and was able to use the images as guiding principles, as he worked with the patients through times of crisis and transformation. It could perhaps be said that the powerful language of alchemy, made largely redundant in terms of actual chemical laboratories in our present age, has surfaced again in the field of psychology, giving this young science vitality and a mythical dimension – it is *almost* as if the images had "a life of their own"!

So it seems that where systems of knowledge touch on the archetypal, they then have a power and create an effect which stretches way beyond the original cultural and historical sphere in which they surfaced. They may take on a timeless quality, something underneath the particular garments in which they are inevitably dressed. The images may seem awesome, even frightening, because they are speaking to a place in us which lies beyond the confines of our personal world. This *may* be perceived as a threat to our identity, or to our values, or to our religion. That is the negative side. The positive is that such images can put us in touch with a kind of knowledge which is not ephemeral, which connects us with other times and places, which cuts through the accumulation of personal theories, desires and wishes, and leads us to a simpler and more fundamental form of truth.

The Tarot – History and Origins

The full set of Tarot cards consists of twenty-two pictorial cards, the "Major Arcana", and fifty-six cards in four suits, known as the "Minor Arcana". These suits – pentacles, cups, swords and wands – correspond to the modern playing-card suits of diamonds, hearts, spades and clubs, but each contains one extra court card (each suit has a Page and a Knight rather than just a Jack). The suits in Tarot are usually associated with the four elements, earth, water, fire and air, and this plays a part in their interpretation. As the Minor Arcana consists of numbered cards and court cards, as opposed to symbolic devices, readings from it tend to be more limited, and mundane – certainly not without value, but secondary to readings from the Major Arcana. There seems to be a wide variety of interpretations for each card.

Attempts have been made to express the Minor Arcana in pictorial form. For instance, there is the popular "Waite" pack, which was chiefly devised by A. E. Waite as part of his work with the occult order "The Golden Dawn" at the beginning of the twentieth century. In this pack the cards reflect the cabbalistic and magical teachings of the Golden Dawn. They are of great interest, if a little lurid in colour and expression, and can be used very effectively, but it should be realised that the pack is only one interpretation of the Minor Arcana rather than a traditional delineation. Even the Waite pack has its own history by now, since the original plates for it were destroyed in World War II and the copies on sale today are an inexact replica of the original sets of cards; if one has the opportunity to examine one of the first, pre-war sets, many more subtleties of symbolism can be detected in the careful detail of the pictures.

Much interest can be gained from studying and using the Minor Arcana, as it gives scope for interpreting the meaning of numbers and elements, and there is room for considerable freedom of personal opinion. However, it is of a different order from the twenty-two picture cards of the Tarot; historically there is no evidence to show that the Major and Minor Arcana originated together, although they have often been combined effectively in the last few hundred years. Those wishing to use the Minor Arcana in conjunction with the Tarot trumps will find plenty of literature available to help them. The rest of this chapter will concentrate on the Major Arcana.

Much has been written and surmised about the origin of the Major Arcana. You may read that it comes from Egypt, from India, from the gypsies, maybe even from outer space. But there is no firm evidence for any of this. The simple facts are that the Tarot cards were first known in France, in the fourteenth century, and soon spread to other European countries, especially Italy, Switzerland and Germany. They were produced in many forms, some of the earliest being large, exquisitely painted cards commissioned for royalty and aristocracy, while the more popular varieties were crude but striking woodcuts used by itinerant fortune-tellers. In conjunction with the Minor Arcana, these were also used for gaming. (In Italy you may still have your fortune read in the traditional manner with the Tarot, and buy packs of *Tarocci* from newsagents to indulge in gambling games. England does not have a long or strong tradition of Tarot reading, and tended to use ordinary playing cards for fortune-telling until the middle of the twentieth century.)

The twenty-two cards do indeed call up echoes of places and times other than Europe in the Middle Ages. But when the images are studied carefully, it will be found that they have a strange assortment of affinities – to Middle Eastern and classical mythology, to medieval morality emblems, to Mithraic and even pagan Bronze Age symbolism. Some authors on the Tarot can even discern Buddhist images in the cards, although these are unlikely to have direct historical associations. Taken altogether, the Major Arcana has a late medieval gloss to it, yet is oddly elusive if one tries to find a single source for its emblems. What does this signify? As I discuss each individual card, I will give examples of the resonances it has with different mythologies and cultures; there is no doubt at all that many of the separate symbols on the cards existed before the Tarot pack as a whole was first known. My own view on the Tarot is that it was probably put together by a person, or, more likely, a group of people, who wanted to put out a system of knowledge into the world in an attractive and potentially popular form. To do this, they chose symbols which had immediate significance, drawing partly from the common stock of religious or mythological imagery, perhaps partly from their own imaginative understanding.

The symbols are more than a mere collection of cards, though, for they make a structured whole. Their number is twenty-two in all, which corresponds to the number of letters in the Hebrew alphabet and to the paths on the Cabbalistic Tree of Life. This ancient and diagrammatic way of mapping the creation of the world was originally an expression of mystical Judaism, but entered the Western world in medieval times, becoming a strong influence upon bodies such as the Neo-Platonic Florentine Academy in the Renaissance, and later inspiring the work of William Blake, the artist, and W. B. Yeats, the poet. The Hebrew letters are closely associated with the Tree of Life, and as twenty-two is a number not commonly found in other philosophical systems, except in Indian music, it is quite likely that the originators of the Tarot had this mystical structure in mind. Both the Hebrew alphabet and the Cabbalistic Tree of Life are considered a complete system of knowledge in their own right, reflecting the essential manifestations of the Divine in the human world. Naturally enough, this association has not escaped students of the Tarot, and it is common practice to assign letters of the Hebrew alphabet, and paths upon the Tree, to the cards.

Let us suppose, then, that the creators of the Tarot wished to put out their knowledge in popular form. They have an overall structure (which we shall look at more closely), a set of fascinating, enigmatic symbols, some familiar, some more obscure, and, as a vehicle to take them out into the world, card games – the latest craze in medieval times. The symbols are beautiful enough for kings and princes to treasure, profound enough for philosophers to use, and sharply defined enough for the eventual production of cheaper woodcuts which the general populace could purchase for divination or gambling, according to their inclinations. As I said earlier: this is my own theory. But whatever the origins of the cards, it is clear that the Tarot is a remarkable device. It has enough symbolic interest to have been studied now for six hundred years. It has enough popular appeal to be perpetuated as a game. It has enough flexibility, self-consistency and variety to be used as an extremely effective form of divination.

Whether it was originally used as a method for divination, we cannot know for sure. But perhaps this is a twentieth-century way of approaching the question, for in earlier times divination and philosophy were not entirely separate activities. The search for knowledge included both these endeavours. Reason, speculation and imagination are the human faculties used – or which *should* be used – in both. At any rate, a tradition of using the Tarot pack for divination has come down to us. The cards themselves have been produced in great variety. Even the early packs may depict the symbols in different ways. When I describe the "traditional" pack in detail below, this is the usual blueprint for Tarot packs, but the reader should bear in mind that many minor and even gross variations may appear in cards now in museums or selling in shops today. There is something about the Tarot that makes people want to try to represent it in their own way.

The Structure of the Pack

The twenty-two cards of the Tarot are usually numbered from one to twenty-one, with one card, The Fool, designated as 0. The numbering and ordering are traditional, although it is uncertain if the very earliest cards were numbered. There is plenty of room for exploring the symbolism of the number attached to each card, as well as for making cross-connections to the Hebrew alphabet and the Tree of Life. As this topic has been dealt with at considerable length by other writers, I shall make only one suggestion here as to how one might look at the structure. That is: the twenty-one numbered cards can be seen as three cycles of seven, forming one large cycle whose central point is designated by the "0" card, The Fool.

The cards in the first cycle, The Magician, The High Priestess, The Empress, The Emperor, The Hierophant, The Lovers and The Chariot, can be viewed as cards of "being". We can become any one of those characters, express the drives they represent, and assume their roles. They have a simplicity of intention and a personal power which equates with basic human drives. The second cycle contains Justice, The Hermit, The Wheel of Fortune, Strength, The Hanged Man, Death and Temperance. These can be interpreted as cards of interaction; the emphasis is on how we respond to the world, balance its energies, adjust to its demands. All these cards represent a choice, a way in which we can act in handling situations. The final cycle comprises The Devil, The Tower (or House of God), The Star, Judgement, The Moon, The Sun and The World. With this cycle the emphasis seems to shift on to external forces which affect us. These may be "higher energies", in the sense of spiritual influences, or may be mundane or physical in their origin. Looking at the three cycles in this way, we can say that the first is, in a sense, the most simple and the last the most complicated. In the first cycle, different simple modes of being are expressed, in the second the relationship between oneself and the world, and in the last the reality of events and forces affecting one from outside. The Fool is first and last, carrying all knowledge or no knowledge at all.

The main purpose of studying the numbering of the Tarot is that we should begin to see interconnections between the cards. It is like building up a delicate network of complex pathways, a web that we can use when we take up the cards for divination. Some people may prefer to keep to one system of numbering symbolism, and one set of core definitions for the Tarot, and build their interpretations upon that. Others will be eager to look at the pack in every way that they can, and use this fluidity to give them freedom of movement in divination. Every practitioner needs to take time to become familiar with the pack and its symbols, however, for the emblems on the cards have a universality that will speak to us, if we first allow our own personal associations and impressions to settle. If we plunge straight into readings with the Tarot without this initial preparation, then at best such readings will be psychically inspired, and at worst products of our distorted imagination. The Tarot is a language; take time to explore its vocabulary.

The Individual Cards

1. THE MAGICIAN

A young man with a broad hat stands in front of a table, on which are laid out cups, balls, a knife and other tools of the trade. He holds up a magician's wand.

The Magician, or Juggler, was a popular figure in late medieval and Renaissance times. The image on the card is how he was commonly portrayed, with his simple magical paraphernalia, and a cloth on the table to deaden the noise as he performed tricks of illusion to delight the gathered crowd. The medieval juggler was a travelling man, sometimes involved with selling medicine and giving out stories and songs as well.

The Magician is the master of creation, and the master of illusion. The card represents the tapping of energy, and the directing of it with precision and skill. To keep this flow of creation going, however, one has to recognise that all the things one can achieve in this world are, ultimately, games and illusions. The Magician knows how to make the best of all opportunities that each moment affords.

The card can signify inspiration, which seems to come out of thin air, like the balls which The Magician produces. It can indicate a flair for business and for making money. In some cases it may mean deceit, trickery, or even being caught on the sharp edge of one's own cleverness. It is a card of wit, humour and impulse.

2. THE HIGH PRIESTESS

A woman with a tall headdress sits before a veil or curtain hung between two pillars, holding an open book upon her lap.

This is a hard image to fix, historically. Sometimes she is called Juno, or The Female Pope. In a thirteenth-century illustration, older than the earliest existing Tarot cards, a composite image of this and The Hierophant (no. 5) appears under the name of "Prudence": a female crowned figure is shown instructing a crowd of respectful supplicants from an open scroll. Plainly, the creators of the Tarot wished to include the image of a female spiritual mentor, in a society where acceptable images for this were in short supply.

This card is an emblem of knowledge and understanding. It signifies innate knowledge, rather than book learning, and points to the kind of understanding that grows through experience, whether individual or collective. It may suggest the need to rely more on one's inner resources and to use silence wisely. The High Priestess herself can be seen as the keeper of the mysteries, and is connected with the practice of religion and meditation.

Where this card occurs in a reading for a woman, it may mean that she can trust her own judgement. For a man, it advises taking a more intuitive approach rather than relying on clever ideas or external opinions. For both, it is a symbol of patience and of allowing the natural momentum of events to build up, rather than forcing the pace.

3. THE EMPRESS

As The High Priestess is the woman of inner life, so The Empress is the woman of the world. She sits enthroned, carrying a shield and bearing a sceptre. Sometimes the shield is emblazoned with an eagle. Her image is more straightforward, and does not seem to set us so many historical puzzles. It is possible that she and The Emperor have a connection with the allegorical King and Queen of alchemy, who symbolise, among other things, gold and silver. She portrays the principle of female energy at work in the world. At the physical level this can suggest pregnancy or sexuality. On the emotional it represents protection, nourishment and motherhood; it may signal over-dependence on another person, or over-indulgence of personal feelings. The Empress also has an air of authority about her, showing confidence in her own powers. As with all the seven cards of "being", this personal authority has to be exercised with discretion, or it may grow into conceit and self-satisfaction.

The fruitfulness of The Empress may signify a project about to come to life.

4. THE EMPEROR

He is seated, usually seen in profile, with the trappings of his office, a sceptre and a shield. As with The Empress, the shield may bear the image of an eagle. It is possible that this may be the eagle of Jove and that the sceptre held by The Emperor is akin to the lightning bolts grasped by the god. This association is not unique to the Tarot and has been used on royal and imperial insignia since Roman times.

The card signifies the enacting of will. A firm will has a quiet but powerful authority, knowing its aims and relying on indwelling strength to see them accomplished. The Emperor does not have to rise from his throne to give his orders and set them in motion. The card may be a warning as to the strength of one's own power, and a reminder to use it justly and sparingly. It may represent destiny, or a path that has been chosen. As a father figure, The Emperor carries the qualities of detached love. This love can be stern as well as compassionate, and reveal itself as anger when appropriate.

5. THE HIEROPHANT

In his papal tiara, The Pope is seated before two pillars, his left hand holding the staff with three crosses, his right hand blessing the small figures who kneel in front of him. The pillars are further behind than they are with The High Priestess.

The depiction of a religious or teaching figure as much larger than the followers sitting or kneeling in front seems to have been a common medieval or Renaissance device. It emphasises the link between pupil and master, considered a highly important one at this period in history. Indeed, the physical arrangement for the passing on of knowledge was symbolic in itself. In the early medieval Arab schools the great teachers would form the centre of a circle, their most experienced students made the inner circle and the novices would be on the outer periphery. It was the job of the older students to relay the teachings back to the younger ones.

The Hierophant and The High Priestess are both cards about knowledge, but the difference is this: she is in direct contact with the pillars and the veil, sometimes interpreted as the Holy Temple; The Pope is some distance away. He brings through knowledge so that it can be voiced and given to others. He uses active intellect in formulating ideas and his powers of communication are greater, his instruction more explicit. This is a card of teaching, listening and learning. In its less favourable aspects, the image can signify being too dependent upon advice or upon ritual and convention.

6. THE LOVERS

A young man stands between two women, gazing at one, with

his arm around the other. Above him hovers a winged Cupid pointing an arrow directly towards his heart.

This is an interesting card, whose image appears to have evolved through time. In early versions of the Tarot the card shows a pair, or several pairs, of lovers underneath a canopy surmounted by one or more Cupids. In the common representation that has come down to us, however, there is clearly some sort of a decision being made. In *Orbis Sensualium Pictus*, by Comenius (1658), the same picture appears as an illustration of the struggle of choosing between virtue and vice, and it is entitled "Moral Philosophy".

In interpretation, therefore, we have the straightforward signs of being smitten by love, but also the implication that to follow any such inclinations of the heart involves a choice. By choosing one, the other must be rejected. The lover hesitates, wanting to have all that he has had before, but desiring a new love for the future too. Thus the card may point to a love affair, or to a choice to be made, or indeed to both. It signifies the strength of desire that is within us, the love of life that wells up continually and manifests itself in many different ways. Our progress through life is marked by many choices, some of them made even before we are aware of it.

7. THE CHARIOT

The crowned and armed youth stands in a covered chariot pulled by two horses. This is the triumphal car, a classical Roman emblem of victory.

The card denotes energy and drive. It signifies achievement and the overcoming of obstacles, sometimes through battle. The harnessing of the horses can be seen as the controlling of one's own emotional power. Feelings such as anger, desire and excitement make terrible masters but excellent servants. The driver does not seem to have reins, perhaps indicating that once emotions are understood and put to work productively, instinct, feeling and rational consciousness are capable of moving forward together in harmony, without overt control. But he wears armour, showing that protection is often necessary since blind trust may come to grief. He is independent, self-contained, alert and prepared. But the Charioteer, if wrongly motivated, can be cruel and proud and ride rough-shod over others. The Chariot is very similar in interpretation to Mars, astrologically – a driving force which, correctly handled, can achieve great things, but which, if badly controlled, can be reckless and harmful.

8. JUSTICE

The female figure of Justice sits with the sword pointing upwards in her right hand and the scales balanced from her left.

This is another image whose roots are in Roman culture, which first associated Justice with a pair of scales. Our Tarot figure of Justice remains open-eyed, true to its medieval portrayal, since the image of Justice blindfold did not become current until the sixteenth century. Justice is one of the four cardinal virtues, a schema originating in Platonic thought and taken up by the Christian Church. Of the other three, Temperance already has a place in the Tarot pack, and in certain variations upon the standard pack, Fortitude and Prudence are also shown.

This card may be a straightforward indication of legal matters, but it also represents the laws operating in our own lives. Justice is a fact, for as we sow, we reap. Knowing of what kind the seeds are, how to sow them, and how to cultivate, is a science that we can pursue, however. If we can understand principle, then our scope for applying it extends. The chef who understands the principles of cake-making can invent any number of delicious confections; the rest of us can only work to fixed recipes. Recognising the law of gravity and discovering the principles of aero-dynamics has enabled us to override the pull of the earth and fly in planes and rockets. The same idea is valid in our personal lives, where a knowledge of our own strengths and weaknesses can help us to use them productively. The card Justice points to the pattern of cause and effect, and invites us to learn its laws.

9. THE HERMIT

A side-view of a robed and bearded man who stands holding up a lantern in one hand and leaning on a stick held in the other.

The Hermit has been a significant figure in Christian life since the early centuries AD. Just as our Hermit is shown in a monk's robe, so monks and hermits have been closely connected at different times, hermits taking on monastic orders and monks setting out to become contemplative hermits. The lantern may relate to Diogenes, the Greek philosopher, as he was often depicted holding up a lamp in broad daylight in his search for an honest man.

This image represents a quest, or a personal journey. Often, to further a quest, something must be renounced, and so this may be a card of giving up unnecessary encumbrances. The Hermit has the power to see things plainly, without glamour, and thus may signify honesty and simplicity. He knows his life is a small flame, like the one in his lamp, and that an unmeasured vastness lies beyond it. The card can show the emerging of the true self, the willingness to give up pretence, or the desire to be alone.

10. THE WHEEL OF FORTUNE

A spoked wheel revolves, suspended in a wooden frame. On top sits a crowned animal-like figure; another is rising to take his place at the top, while a third plunges down where the wheel turns under.

The goddess Fortuna and her wheel have been the subject of much speculation and artistic endeavour since classical times. It is likely that our own "Big Wheel" at the fair, and the lottery wheel, were invented as direct representations of the fickle deity. There are many representations of her wheel from medieval times and earlier; it is sometimes depicted with smaller wheels inside the greater – "wheels within wheels". Fortuna was originally associated with destiny, not chance, and the turnings of her wheel were used as an emblem by those who described the ways in which people might rise and fall in their lives.

The interpretation of the card is thus self-evident. It can symbolise the arrival of unexpected luck – of either kind. It can imply that one is bound to the general cycle of ups and downs, and might try learning to follow one's own destiny – the handle to turn the wheel is ready and available for use. It suggests that success should not be clung to, nor failure regarded as permanent, as there is constant movement in life. Routine is indicated, and sometimes the card signifies that one must go round on the treadmill for a while longer before moving to a more interesting phase.

11. STRENGTH

A woman, wearing a long, flowing dress and a broad-brimmed hat, stands over a lion and holds its jaws apart.

This association of a woman with wild animals, and in particular with lions, goes far back in human history. The "Mistress of the Beasts" was represented in ancient civilisations such as Crete, Phoenecia and Mesopotamia by statues and paintings where she may be seen standing between lions, upon a lion's back, or in a chariot drawn by lions. In an Italian illustration contemporary with early Tarot she sits with a lion nestling against her and she is stroking an ox. The powerful image of a woman acquiring dominance over these strong and dangerous animals has held sway in our human imagination for a very long time. Some researchers think that even the original domestication of animals may have been initiated by huntsmen bringing home cubs and calves and other baby creatures for the women to rear.

The strength shown, therefore, has an extraordinary power, since it overcomes danger through gentleness, patience and persistence. The woman does not force apart the lion's jaws; the lion, rather, sits in submission and allows her to place her hands at the source of the greatest potential danger, upon its teeth. The interpretation is thus of a strength that works through anything that is *not* direct force – through confidence, compassion, understanding, quietness, maybe even magic. Such strength can only become supreme when the nature of one's opponent is known, and then the opposing force itself can be tamed, rather than destroyed.

12. THE HANGED MAN

A man is shown hanging upside-down, his feet tied to a cross pole and his hands held behind his back. Sometimes he is shown with his hands holding weights, or with money falling out of his pockets.

This card often alarms newcomers to the Tarot, probably because of its name. But if the image is looked at properly, it can at once be seen that the man is not hanging from his neck at all, like an executed criminal. He is suspended from his feet, and – if you turn the card the other way up – he looks quite happy! There are two historical images relevant to this card. Firstly, there is the rather shadowy mythical attribution of the Norse god Odin's ordeal when he hung upside-down from the sacred world tree in order to gain divine knowledge. Such a reversal, or otherwise temporary imprisonment, are common in shamanic traditions, where the candidate must be completely removed from the ordinary sphere of life to gain the essential visions. It is these visions that he will use, to cure or prophesy in his future work. The second image suggests that The Hanged Man is, in fact, an acrobat. There are accounts from Greek and medieval times of how travelling gymnasts would perform acrobatic feats while suspended from a rope or cross pole. In Strutt's *Sports and Pastimes* there is an account of "rope-dancing from the battlements of St Paul's" in 1456: "Then took he the rope and tied it to the cable, and hung by one leg in a certain space, and after recovered himself again with the said rope and unknit the knot and came down again."

Here, then, we have our acrobat and/or shaman – *not* our criminal or suicide. In fact, the ideas of acrobat and shaman combine well, for both are entrusting themselves to a reversal. The acrobat must simply trust his skill and balance, and the strength of the rope. The shaman goes willingly into the unknown, ready to be shaped by what he encounters there. The Hanged Man is thus a card of faith – perhaps not blind faith, but a calculated risk. In the performing arts there comes a point where, having built up techniques, one has to let go, to trust that it will work as it should, and face the immediacy of the performance itself.

13. DEATH

A skeleton with a scythe razes the ground, where severed heads, hands and feet lie among flowers and grass.

We have no trouble recognising the image of Death the Reaper. Medieval illustrations frequently showed him thus, or as riding a white horse and trampling down kings and queens, according to the vision of John in the Book of Revelation: "And I looked, and behold a pale horse: and his name that sat on him was Death . . ." (Chapter 6 v8).

Like The Hanged Man, Death has gained a reputation for bringing dismay and despair within a Tarot reading. But the paradox of death is its fertility. Old plants provide sustenance for new ones. When something is destroyed, there is greater potential for new life. This is apparent at the winter solstice when, although the ground is bare and there is least daylight, we know that the days will now begin to lengthen and plants to grow. The symbol is an expansive one, and does not really imply the bitter finality that it is often taken to represent. Death means change; while this can be a most positive omen, it has to be remembered, of course, that change can be of many kinds, sometimes causing acute anxiety as old patterns are broken up to make way for the new. It is also possible to be addicted to change for its own sake, and so the card could be a warning not to be ruled simply by the desire to destroy the old and make a new start. Death shows that nothing is lost, only transformed. However dead the past may seem, it provides the living basis, and the fertile ground for one's future life.

14. TEMPERANCE

A winged female figure stands holding two jugs, pouring water from one to another. Her appearance seems to be half angelic, half human, and she sometimes has a flower or star upon her brow.

The card Temperance is a stock-in-trade representation of this cardinal virtue. She may pour from one vessel to another as a symbol of diluting wine with water, the moderating of alcohol being one of her influences. But the image may have other connotations: her wings may indicate a role as the "Angel of Time", their swift beating announcing the fleeting passage of time in human life; and the action of her pouring may hark back to Assyrian reliefs and figures of deities pouring out divine water, sometimes directly upon the earth, sometimes, as here, into another receptacle. We must not get too carried away with possibilities of more remote origins however. This is predominantly a medieval emblem, although it is true that in the Tarot it seems to have the bristling edge of Christian virtue smoothed down in its portrayal and is given a gleam of other-worldly beauty.

In interpretation, the card can denote balance and moderation. It can also show the cycles in operation in our lives, for the visual effect of the image is that we see the water as flowing backwards and forwards between the two jugs, rather than always from one to the other. Cycles are to do with the giving out and the replenishing of energy. Knowing which phase of the cycle we are in helps us to use that energy effectively and in proper measure. A "tempering" of effort creates its own beauty. The perpetual motion suggested by the symbol may also be relevant in a reading, suggesting anything from a vacillating instability to an influx of new movement and vitality.

15. THE DEVIL

The Devil in the traditional woodcut pack is a slightly comic figure, being a rather squat hairy devil, complete with horns and leathern wings. He stands on a raised plinth, which has two smaller devils chained to its base. In some packs additional faces with gaping mouths are placed in the devils' chests or stomachs.

As we know, the depiction of the devil was of great interest in medieval society, which concerned itself with the sharp division between good and evil, heaven and hell. Apparently, the grotesque nature of the devil's representation came originally from the Persians and Egyptians, via Byzantine art, and was further embellished by the efforts of medieval monks. By the fifteenth century, his image was declining in popularity, if such a word can be used. Here, then, we have a symbol central to medieval thought, depicted in medieval style, but which could, according to individual theories of the Tarot's origin, be held to derive from a more ancient source.

It might seem unwise to treat this devil in a slightly mocking fashion, but, in fact, there is precedent for this, too. The medieval monks who illuminated so many magnificent manuscripts frequently chose to invest their devils and demons with humour and ridiculous antics. To laugh at him can sometimes be a way of cutting him down to size. A devil ignored or blindly attacked can grow into enormous proportions, as can a devil given too much importance. We don't use the term "devil" very much in our lives any more. Instead, the common parlance may be "bad habits", "negative emotions" and "obsession".

The other important aspect of this card is that it is one of bondage to the principle of necessity. There are, very definitely, times when our choice is limited. If you specialise in any field, your future choices are inevitably limited. If you buy a second car, you have two sets of garage and insurance bills and a double worry on the road. "Take what you want, and pay the price," goes the saying; The Devil is a reminder of the bill that must be paid.

16. THE TOWER

Lightning strikes the top of a tower, ripping off its roof. Showers of stones fall through the sky and figures tumble down to the ground.

The most likely explanation for this image is that it is derived from the Biblical story of the Tower of Babel. Men, trying to build a tower that would reach heaven, had their edifice shattered by the wrath of God for such impudence, and henceforth spoke in many different languages and could no longer understand one another. But like other "stock" images of the Tarot, it seems to have a character of its own as well as employing standard symbolism. A very similar picture is found over a hundred years before the first extant Tarot pack; called "Pride", it shows a King falling or suspended from the pinnacle of a tower. But this is not the Tower of Babel, for three ladies watch him from little windows under the turrets.

This card shows the overthrow of pride, conceit, and secure opinions. Anything built up to a height subjects itself to the law that lightning strikes the highest point. It brings a shock, perhaps totally unexpected. Yet this card can also point to a welcome release from a state of imprisonment; fairy tales are full of wistful maidens longing to be let out of the towers in which they have been locked up. It can indicate a revelation. After lightning has struck, nothing will ever be quite the same again.

17. THE STAR

A beautiful naked woman kneels by the side of a pool, pouring water from two jugs. Above her, one large and seven small stars shine. On a tree in the background sits a bird.

This card is perhaps the most fascinating in the whole pack in respect of its origins. The strange set of symbols only begins to make sense if we look at the collection of myths surrounding the related goddesses Ishtar and Anahita from Babylonia and Iran. Ishtar is known as "The Star of Lamentation"; Anahita is the goddess of the heavenly waters that flow from the region of Venus among the stars. In one of the central myths of Ishtar, she decides to penetrate to the centre of the underworld to fetch the water of life to restore her dead lover, Tammuz. She passes through seven gateways, one of her jewelled adornments being stripped from her at each, until she arrives naked at the sacred pool. In this underworld the souls of the dead are represented by birds. Here, then, we have all the elements of the Tarot card "The Star". And this card, more than all the others, suggests that the creator(s) of the Tarot wove together elements from myths both ancient and modern, for this particular image is not, as far as I know, current in medieval art.

In principle, The Star is a card of generosity and compassion. It may symbolise the heart of the matter, the point at which there is no further secrecy or pretence; the figure is naked and exposed. The card also has connotations of magic, in the sense that the beauty of a starlit night is magical – with a poetic, delicate quality that has to be handled carefully. It can be a card of sympathy and of healing, and, in excess, denote lack of discretion through the tendency to "pour everything out". It may suggest an inner journey, as opposed to The Chariot, which can indicate outer forms of travel.

18. THE MOON

A large, rayed moon with a "man in the moon" countenance shines over a landscape flanked by two towers. Drops fall from the sky onto two dogs who bay up at the moon, and in the foreground a crayfish or lobster rises up through the water.

Occultists may have a field day with this card, drawing parallels with the pagan moon goddess, sacred "yods" falling from the sky (the drops resembling the first letter of the Hebrew name of God), the towers being the portals of Hades or pillars of an Egyptian temple of mysteries, and so on. All or none of this may be deliberately intended. My own research adds two more arrows to the quiver: firstly, that certain Babylonian boundary stones show a crescent moon associated with towers, beasts and a crayfish; and secondly, that the early religious cult of Mithraism, in which mysteries of initiation played a vital part, placed strong emphasis on the heavenly bodies and also used the symbols of dog and scorpion (similar in appearance, of course, to the crayfish). Visitors to Venice may be struck, too, by a resemblance of the towers in The Moon to those of the medieval Arsenal, which guard another watery domain, standing on either side of a major canal at the entrance to the sea lagoon in the Adriatic, in which the island-city lies.

It is not inappropriate that the origins of The Moon should prove so confusing, for it is a card of illusion and of changing images. It represents the power of the imagination, which may entrap us, for in crossing the border into the sub-conscious we may become ensnared by the fascination of its images and fantasies, and lose touch with reality. Hence we have tales of men and women being taken down to fairyland, and who, once they had eaten or drunk of fairy provisions, could not escape again except with outside help. The card can thus signify the personal, subjective element in our lives. It is powerful, emotional, magnetic, and needs to be met with clarity and a certain amount of detachment.

19. THE SUN

Two naked children stand in front of a wall beneath the sun's rays, with drops of light falling around them.

Such an image is recognised as dating from very early times. In their book, *Chariot of the Sun*, Gelling and Davidson state that in the Bronze Age the image of twins, apparently associated with the sun, was of great significance. The twins were shown as two male figures, standing side by side, sometimes holding axes. The authors go on to describe the continuation of this image in classical and Mithraic culture. Here, then, we have a symbol of very ancient origin, common until the early Christian era, but not, apparently, in medieval times. We therefore have representations in the Tarot of Star, Moon and Sun cults, their roots going way back in time, and their authors apparently drawing deliberately upon this ancient heritage.

The card can be seen as the presence of creative energy, love and joy. It has a simplicity, even a naivety about it, for the children play artlessly and unclad in the sun's warmth. It can be a card of sheer pleasure or of serious creative endeavour. It can represent animal high spirits, and excess of enthusiasm. But The Sun, as opposed to The Moon, is straightforward in its attributions and its simplicity should be valued.

20. JUDGEMENT

An angel blowing a trumpet has appeared in the sky. Below, naked figures rise out of their graves and clasp their hands in worship. Here we are back to a familiar medieval emblem portraying the last judgement, when the trumpet awakens the sleeping dead and summons them to heaven.

This card shows a stirring and quickening of life. What seemed to be dead is shown to live. It can represent awakening in any sphere, either when we are alerted by something outside ourselves, or else when we have that effect upon another person. It may thus represent an impulse, a message or a surprise. But it is called "Judgement" – after the first awakening come trials and tests. The writer's inspiration has to go a long way before it becomes a book, and the excitement of a new love affair has to endure much weathering if it is to be a lasting relationship. The trumpet of the angel promises new life, but the judgement of truth, too.

21. THE WORLD

The central image is that of a naked female dancer, carrying a baton in each hand and with only a long scarf draped over her shoulder. She is surrounded by an oval wreath of leaves, and in each of the four corners a symbol representing one of the Four Evangelists is set – angel, eagle, ox and lion.

This is a curious juxtaposition of symbols. As far as I can discover, the oval leafy frame and the images of the Four Evangelists in the corners usually provided the setting for a central figure of Christ. This emblem was then known as "Christ in Glory", and is found from the early medieval period, if not before. But here Christ has been replaced – deliberately? – by a naked dancing girl. She appears to correspond to the classical "salatrix" described in Rich's *Dictionary of Greek and Roman Antiquities*: such figures are "mostly furnished with a large and transparent drapery ... which is sometimes ... entirely removed from the figure and carried floating in the air so as to leave the body altogether exposed to the gaze of the spectators". The salatrix was "a dancing girl ... of indifferent morals but considerable personal beauty".

The reader may like to ponder on this unusual combination of symbols. It seems to give us a meaning for The World which is both male and female, sacred and secular, set together in a way that could be seen either as irreverent or as powerful, according to one's views. It seems to marry elements from each pole of experience, and suggest union and completeness; it is the last numbered card in the pack. Sometimes it may refer to a material and mundane level of existence. At others it may remind us of the beauties to be found in the commonplace, and be an encouragement to search for the divine in our everyday lives. It is reminiscent of the Cabbalistic "Shekinah", the grace of God as it descends to humanity, symbolised by the beauty of woman. The appearance of The World may be a sign of needing to keep one's feet more firmly on the ground. It may suggest a course that has reached its fulfilment and natural end.

0. THE FOOL

A traditionally dressed fool, in cap and bells, strides off with a bundle dangling from a stick hoisted over his shoulder, a staff in his hand, and a small dog jumping up at him from behind.

The card for The Fool appears to be a combination of the

usual image of the court fool, or jester, and that of the beggar, who is often shown ragged, with his staff and dog, wandering from place to place.

Here is the central card of the wheel, the card that has no place in the numberings and structures of the other twenty-one. The Fool is the blind spot of our nature – we can see ahead, and behind, but can never quite make out where we are. He is the human element of the pack – that "human error" factor that turns up in any project or experiment. He is none of the other cards, but contains their potentialities within him unrecognised. The Fool is always travelling. He can be perfectly innocent, or perfectly ignorant, depending upon how you look at him, but he is there within all of us.

In this chapter, I have tried to give an analysis, both in history and in terms of meaning, of a complete divination system. The Tarot is very rich in its symbolism, and its cards are rewarding to study in their own right. What I have given here is, however, only an outline; whole chapters could be written about each card, and the student of the Tarot will have many ideas of his or her own to add to those which I have suggested. With a system such as the Tarot, there are certain central meanings to which one can point, but the individual will fill these out from personal insights which arise either through contemplating the cards, or through the process of divination itself.

It is easy to see that the Tarot is quite a fluid system of divination; the separate cards have ruling principles but many specific applications, and the possibilities of meaning when one starts combining the cards in a lay-out are surely infinite. Unfortunately, there is not the space in this present book to include methods of reading the Tarot through laying out the cards and dealing with them in combination, but once again, the reader is recommended to further literature on the subject for more advice on the matter. What I have endeavoured to do here is to interest the reader who has not encountered the Tarot before, showing what potential depth it has, and to give the reader familiar with the cards, it is hoped, some fresh insights as to their historical associations and interpretation.

Chapter 4

Questions and Answers

Finding the Question

A divination reading only comes into being as a response to a question. Such a question may be posed by the diviner himself, or by a querent seeking the diviner's help; it may be specific or implicit; it may be presented after careful consideration or on the spur of the moment. Before any reading can take place, it must be decided whether the question is valid, and if it can be dealt with by the system of divination at hand. The diviner must also consider his own responsibilities in the matter, and whether he chooses to undertake a reading.

First, let us look at the nature of specific questions. These usually centre round the eternal human preoccupations of love, money, health, length of life, and personal success. It is as well for the diviner to keep this in mind, for often a person requesting a reading may be tempted to couch the question in a lofty expression, nervous of revealing the issue that really matters. Thus, "How do you see my life developing?" or "What are my current chances of happiness?" may in fact mean "Will I get the job I'm applying for?" or "Is my boyfriend going to stay with me?" To obtain an effective reading, the question should be defined as clearly as possible before starting. Question and answer are like arrow and target; they must be aligned before the bow is drawn back.

In subject matter there is really no limit to the type of specific question that can be asked. But there are limitations to the amount of detail that can be expected in response to a specific question. No hard-and-fast guidelines can be given as to the amount of information that a divination reading can supply; it depends upon the question, the method used, and the way in which the diviner likes to work. In general, though, the greater the amount of precise information given, the greater the likelihood of inaccuracy. Divination may reach to a core of truth, whose exact manifestations are hard to plot.

Answers to questions which ask for details of timing are notoriously unreliable. There are methods both in Tarot and in horary astrology, for instance, to determine when an event is likely to take place, but these somewhat rigid and mechanical rules cannot be relied upon, although there are instances where the answers given can be surprisingly accurate. It has already been suggested that, through the process of divination, we enter a different order of time and space; this being so, it can be particularly difficult to frame the knowledge that is gained through divination in terms of time as we experience it at the everyday level.

If a question needs to be well-defined, then why is it that astrologers, palmists and the like are able to give more general readings by looking at their clients' birthcharts or hands? In such general readings implicit questions already exist. These are likely to be "What kind of a person am I?", "What does the future hold for me?" or "What is my present condition?" The structure of the divinatory method may also have questions implied within it which are helpful in giving a well-rounded and balanced reading. The twelve houses of the horoscope in astrology, for instance, define the main areas of life, which can all receive a measure of interpretation as the chart is read. The first house answers questions about the type of environment the person prefers, the second about money, the fifth lovers and children, and so on. These in-built categories of question are also an aid to correcting any imbalance in the diviner's own interests; if the astrologer faithfully considers all twelve houses, he or she is prevented from letting personal fixations – whether on money, lovers or whatever! – predominate. Even with implicit questions, though, it is worthwhile for the diviner and the querent to make sure that they understand one another. If the astrologer's primary interest in studying a chart is to answer the question: "What sort of a person am I?" and the client wants to know: "What does the future hold for me?", then mutual dissatisfaction may well result. Diviner and querent should be attuned to one another, although retaining their separate identities, as we shall see later.

Before a reading begins, therefore, the diviner needs to be clear in mind as to its aim, and should decide whether the question is acceptable. Although questions can relate to just about any aspect of life, it does not follow that it is appropriate to answer any question. Divination involves a partnership, and it is only effective when there is good intent and commitment on both sides. Horary astrologer Derek Appleby defines it thus:

> Before you even begin to draw a chart, make a definite decision as to whether or not to accept the question. Avoid giving judgement upon frivolous matters, and do not accept questions merely to test your art. The questions should be put in good faith with a genuine desire for serious judgement.
>
> (Derek Appleby, *Horary Astrology*, Aquarian Press, 1985)

The matter enquired about need not be one of life-and-death importance, but the questioner should have a true interest in the matter, and, as far as can be told in advance, be willing to receive an answer even if it does not tally with existing hopes. Most astrologers and diviners have had the frustrating experience of working hard upon a reading, only to have it rejected for the simple reason that it does not match the client's expectations.

Sometimes the questioner may have a sincere interest in his or her question, but the diviner will consider that such curiosity should not be satisfied. Many astrologers will refuse to interpret the chart of a third party without that person's consent; the seeker, for example, may be eager to learn about the inner nature and drives of his girlfriend, or employer, and have obtained their birth data without their agreement that a horoscope should be drawn up. Clearly, this presents ethical problems. Again, many diviners will be very wary of questions about the course of an illness, or how long a person has to live. Such a matter may not be a foregone conclusion, since the person concerned may have some choice in the matter, and even if the outcome should be inevitable, it may not be helpful to know it in advance. The practice of divination presents moral responsibilities.

It is interesting to consider where those responsibilities lie. If a diviner considers that the burden is solely a personal one, then questions are likely to be treated with extreme caution. If it is thought that the method used is the mechanism that produces truth, then the skilled diviner, confident in technique, will approach questions more boldly. But if a diviner is seen as an instrument of a higher power, in the same way as the priestesses of Delphi were seen as the handmaidens of divine Apollo, then the responsibility is taken out of the human level to that of divine will. It would be difficult to justify one approach over the others, totally; each has strengths and weaknesses. But it is certainly advisable to know where you stand, and to take on the discipline of that position.

The practices where the diviner is seen as an instrument of higher power are usually heavily ritualised, so that personal elements are washed away before there is any approach made to divination.

You state that there are many who grasp the future by means of divine possession and divine inspiration and that they are awake as far as their ability to act and their sense perceptions are concerned, but not really conscious or not as conscious as before. I also want to show, in this context, the characteristics of those who are truly possessed by the gods. For if they submit their whole life as a vehicle, as a tool, to the gods who inspire them, they either exchange their human life for a divine life or else they adjust their life to the god and do not act according to their own sense perceptions, nor are they awake like those whose senses are completely awake. They do not perceive the future by themselves, nor do they move like those who act on an impulse. They are not conscious in the way they were before, nor do they concentrate their native intelligence on themselves or manifest any special knowledge.

(Iamblichus, *On the Mysteries of Egypt*, quoted in *Arcana Mundi*, ed. Georg Luck, Johns Hopkins University Press, 1985)

Diviners who consider a reading to be their own responsibility may be more limited in the range of questions they will accept, but they are likely to have a flexible approach denied to those who work by method and rules only. The challenge facing all diviners is to give themselves wholeheartedly to each reading they take on, yet to detach themselves from it afterwards, for their role only lasts as long as the reading does.

We are fortunate today that most people practising divination are allowed to choose whether or not to proceed on a question, and that their lives do not depend upon the answers they give. Touchy Roman emperors were known to order the execution of astrologers whose predictions they disliked. One such story has an unpleasant twist to it. The emperor Domitian arrested an astrologer for unfavourable forecasts, and asked him how he, the astrologer, foresaw his own death. The unhappy man replied that he was destined to be torn apart by dogs. In order to try to discredit his astrology, the emperor ordered that the man be executed and his body disposed of with extreme care; but in the middle of his cremation a hurricane overturned the funeral pyre and a pack of dogs ate the corpse.

Community Divination

So far we have spoken of the diviner as though he or she is always one person reading the signs for a second person. There are variations on this procedure. It has long been the tradition that a divinatory judgement may be sought on the fortunes of the community or nation as a whole, and sometimes several members of the community or an entire group will join in to make the judgement. In Scotland, at Hallowe'en, it was the custom at a local or family gathering to pass round a dish of mashed potatoes, containing various charms. Each person would take a spoonful, and his luck would be judged by any charm he found there, a coin signifying money, a ring a marriage, and so on. In Elizabethan England, guests at a banquet were sometimes served their food on decorative "roundels"; having eaten, the guests were invited to upturn the roundels, and read the fortunes inscribed underneath. No doubt there were occasions where the hostess took some care as to how she planned her seating arrangements. Our modern custom of pulling Christmas crackers and looking for the jokes, mottoes and gifts within is a survival of this community divination practice.

Other practices were more sinister. At Hallowe'en, again, in Wales and Scotland, special bonfires were lit on hilltops, and among the rituals carried out was one where each person placed a marked white stone in the Hallow fire. The next day, these stones were drawn out from the ashes; any that were missing or cracked were tokens of ill luck or even death for their owners. Another occupation in rural villages of Britain was to sit up in the church porch on Midsummer's Eve and watch for apparitions passing into the church, of people in the village who would die during the coming year. It is easy to see how divination and witchcraft could arouse deep suspicion under such circumstances, and become a vehicle for active malevolence. An ill-natured person might choose to try to blight the spirit of another by claiming that his ghost had been seen entering the church. Even when divination itself was the true aim, the seer could find herself accused of causing the death rather than foreknowing it. It is not the purpose of this book to travel far into those dubious areas of cause and effect, but it is worth pointing out that there are aspects of divination which warrant great care. It is wise for the diviner to think through his or her attitudes and to know the responsibilities involved.

Checks and Safeguards

We may at times be our own diviners. Children almost invariably are; whether they are counting plum stones, bus tickets or magpies, it is their own fortune that they are interested in rather than anyone else's. In the adult world it is different. Many of the systems, as I have suggested in Chapter 2, are complex, capable of being interpreted in more than one way and on more than one level, and it is not always possible to have enough objectivity about one's own situation to carry out a personal reading. Our minds leap to details and we pin our hopes and fears on these – if the Death card turns up in a Tarot reading, we expect the worst, despite the fact that the card is also a symbol of rebirth, and if The Lovers is laid out we jump to the conclusion that the current romance will be all right after all, even though the young man in the picture has a lady on either arm! Divination practices require the reading to be seen as a whole before hard-and-fast judgements are made, and it is extremely difficult to put aside all our expectations and approach with an open mind. The I Ching is probably the best divination system in modern use for personal application. Each hexagram is a chapter of philosophy in its own right, and rarely seems to give out quick answers. The questioner must read it through carefully, think it over and absorb its content before seeing how it is likely to apply to the situation enquired about, and by this mental effort he or she stands a better chance of letting go of the strong ideas or feelings that occasioned the reading. It is only by standing back from one's personal involvement that a measure of objectivity can be achieved. If one is prepared to put in this effort when consulting the I Ching, I have found that it rarely disappoints; but if one goes at it demanding an answer, it often appears to give an irrelevant or incomprehensible reading.

Some systems contain their own devices to screen out inappropriate questions or attitudes. The I Ching itself has one hexagram known as "Youthful Folly" whose judgement is:

Youthful folly has success.
It is not I who seek the young fool;
The young fool seeks me.
At the first oracle I inform him.
If he asks two or three times, it is importunity.
If he importunes, I give him no information.
Perseverance furthers.

(*The I Ching*, Richard Wilhelm translation, Routledge and Kegan Paul, 1951)

In one Tarot lay-out, the reading is prevented if The Fool turns up in the first line of six cards. This is said to indicate obstruction coming either from the diviner or from the querent, and both are advised to reconsider their approach, checking that the question is well-formulated and that there are no preconceptions inhibiting the judgement. And in horary astrology, several rules must be applied to a chart when it is first drawn up to check that it is "radical" and may be judged. Saturn appearing in the seventh house, for instance, suggests that the astrologer is not fit to give judgement on this particular occasion. The part of the zodiac "rising" at the beginning of the first house in horary astrology must be at more than 3 and less than 27 degrees of a sign. If the degree of the zodiac that is rising is an early or late one, then it is considered too soon or too late to make any pronouncement on the matter. The purpose of such rules is to prevent a hasty and perhaps ill-thought-out involvement with a question, and where such safeguards are incorporated into a divination system, they are helpful rather than frustrating devices, often preventing subsequent misunderstanding.

The Scope of the Answer

It has been mentioned already that the system of divination used must be in keeping with the information sought, and with the field in which the diviner chooses to operate. A water diviner is not in business to give character readings or advice on human affairs; he is there to seek out water, or perhaps minerals, lying beneath the earth's surface. The technique of dowsing itself, however, can have a wider application, for pinpointing a location, or even for detecting allergies or health problems. One method is to take a hair of the patient and, while keeping in contact with it, see how the pendulum reacts when items of foodstuff are named. If the swing of the pendulum is "negative", then this is taken to suggest an allergic reaction to the food on the part of the patient. But even in this wider use of the dowsing technique, we could not expect to receive a personality profile, nor advice about which course of action to take. Dowsing, as already shown, works by the binary "yes/no" principle, and insight into character or future possibilities is not gained by this. To define personality, for instance, by asking questions such as: "Is he an angry man?" and "Does he like sport?" and receiving "yes" or "no" answers is going to create a caricature, not reveal an identity. For this, a system is needed which has more subtlety, and more room for interpretation.

But dowsing itself is not a "low-grade" divination because it is unsuitable for giving a portrait of human character; it is a method of divination tempered to suit particular purposes, especially where concise, clear and pragmatic results are needed. Its roots are in responses to physical phenomena – the presence of water, or the position of a missing object, for instance – but dowsing techniques have been developed to extend its application to map-reading (as we have already seen) and to answering a surprisingly wide range of questions, some of which appear to transcend the normal boundaries of time. Take, for example, this case history from *Dowsing* by Tom Graves (Turnstone Books, 1976):

> Another friend of mine had to contact a colleague urgently – which would have been simple enough had the colleague not been quite so nomadic. My friend phoned the two numbers he had – 'He hasn't been here for months' and 'Sorry, he left with all his stuff a couple of hours ago.' So he took a pendulum and the A to Z atlas of London, and started on the index map. The pendulum clearly indicated one page, and then one street on that page.... That's better. What kind of a place? A hotel. But which hotel? He hunted out a trade directory, and on the list of hotels for that street his pendulum reacted at once. Is that the right hotel? Yes. So he phoned the hotel and asked if his colleague was there. 'No, sir, no-one of that name here.' But something nagged at him intuitively, and he left a message there, 'just in case.'
>
> Two hours later his colleague rang him from that hotel, somewhat perplexed, and asked him how did he find him, because he'd only decided to go there an hour ago?

Such a test of dowsing plainly pushes that technique to extremes, and we could not normally hope to achieve such spectacular success. Tom Graves adds wisely:

> Now that's an extreme example, but it should give you the general idea. ... Remember that the information you can get from this kind of work is *only* information – untested and unreliable information, not fact. By all means use that information 'on the off-chance', to see if it *is* true, but *never trust it.*

Diviners learn through experience that no system is infallible, and that a useful attitude to cultivate is that of undertaking a reading with commitment, but without firm expectations.

Case histories of divination have rarely been put together and made publicly available, although one may read in texts both ancient and modern of the different techniques which can be used. Some case studies have come to light in manuscripts compiled for private records, and occasionally they may form part of a work intended for general consumption, as we shall see shortly. Records of astrological interpretations are probably better-kept than those of other systems. This may be because early astrology was an official occupation; the royal priests of the ancient Near East had to justify their keep and account for their findings. Astrology has also, from its beginnings, involved research into celestial movements (this later becoming the separate science of astronomy) and calculations, all of which needed to be recorded in the attempt to build up a body of knowledge. As a complex procedure, astrology has largely remained throughout its history in the domain of the literate. Hence its practitioners were more likely to note down their results than the "wise" men and women who read palms, Tarot cards and natural omens, through inherited lore and intuition.

The development of different branches of astrology has come about, it seems, as a response to the different kinds of questions asked and answers required. The first prognostications were for the emperor and the whole nation; they were predictions about peace, war, harvests and government, and were based on quite generalised observations of the skies. The techniques available were not capable of being applied to personal destinies. But around the dawning of the Christian era, the inquisitive nature of the Greeks led to a refining of astronomical techniques so that a complete horoscope as we know it now could be drawn up for a moment of birth, and interpreted for an individual. Some of these early explorations into natal astrology remain:

Sun and Jupiter in Capricorn, Moon and Saturn in Leo, Mars in Pisces, Venus and Ascendent in Scorpio, Mercury in Sagittarius. . . . He was a dancer, and in his twentyfifth year he was put in confinement in the course of a public riot, but he was defended before the governor and released . . . and became more esteemed. . . . The nativity was precarious as regards loss of reputation . . . and danger of life. But Venus being found in the Ascendent . . . and Jupiter with the Sun, it had the best imaginable outcome . . .

(Quoted in *Greek Horoscopes*, O. Neugebauer and H. B. Van Hoesen)

The Greeks developed the idea of a "birth" moment to include the birth of an event, journey or enterprise. They reasoned that if the moment of a human being coming into existence could be charted, then likewise anything arising in a moment would bear its imprint, and any future development could thus be read from the astrological significators. This branch of astrology they called Katarche.

Thus the symbolism of astrology had become rich enough, and the techniques precise enough to be focused on individual forms of life, and questions could now be asked of astrologers regarding personal character and fortune. Using the language of astrology to describe human qualities has remained the chief activity of astrologers to the present day; it is a language admirably suited to answering the questions: "Who am I, and where am I going?" But its symbolism can also be applied to descriptions of events, places, even animals and objects. This is the territory of horary astrology, the art of answering specific questions through a horoscope drawn up for the moment of asking the question.

Before I give some examples of how the language is applied in horary readings, there is a further point to make about the divisions between the branches of astrology. Not many astrologers, either in the past or in the present, have ever spread their efforts over all the possibilities of astrological divination, pronouncing equally on the fate of nations, individual psychology, health, times for planting and sowing, and all manner of human questions. In fact, astrologers not only tend to specialise in one branch of astrology, but may even deny that others have any validity. Natal astrologers have been known to dismiss horary astrology as outmoded superstition, and horary astrologers to see natal astrologers as lacking the guts to make firm judgements on their charts. The basic cause of this is that different methods of astrology are geared up to particular types of questions and their answers. The open-ended, fluid and integrated approach of natal astrology, where planets and signs are judged in relationship to one another, would be hopeless in horary astrology, where the interpreter must work with decisiveness, singling out certain planets for emphasis and consigning the rest into second place. The horoscopes are exactly the same in content and lay-out, but what is relevant in each case is different.

The astrologer, therefore, goes into his or her work knowing what sort of questions are to be dealt with and the kind of answers needed, and this will define the specific techniques of astrology used and the attitude taken. To build up expertise in one mode of operation as an astrologer, it may be necessary for some people to limit the number of techniques used. And in strengthening one's own position, one may be tempted to reject other pictures as invalid. It is a skilled astrologer indeed who can slip from one branch of astrology to another; he or she must not only be familiar with the different methods in use, but be able to drop the attitude appropriate to one and assume that relevant to the other. Such accomplishment demands that the astrologer be not too attached to personal attitudes, treating them as useful, but interchangeable.

The best-known book of "case histories" for horary astrology comes from the pen of William Lilly in his book *Christian Astrology*. Lilly was a seventeenth-century English astrologer, who was consulted by rich and poor alike during his years of practice, even finding himself uncomfortably involved in the Civil War when both sides saw fit to ask his advice! His book is a compound of astrological advice and instructions, illustrated by examples from his own experience. The commonest problems presented to him concerned loss or theft, and it is from this area that some of his most colourful cases come. I think it is worth quoting two examples nearly in full. Readers without specialised knowledge of astrology will not be able to follow all Lilly's reasoning – it is complex enough even for the experienced astrologer! – but the process of converting astrological symbols into precise definitions is clear enough. It is not only clear, but poetic, too, in its unravelling of a heavenly maze into human understanding. Here, first, is Lilly's example of divining for missing small beasts:

A Dogge missing, where?

Living in London where we have few or no small Cattle, as Sheep, Hogs, or the like, as in the Countrey; I cannot give example of such creatures, onely I once set the Figure preceding concerning a Dogge (who is in the nature of small Beasts) which Dogge was fled and missing. The Quere unto me was, 'What part of the City they should search, next if he should ever recover him.'

The Querent was signified by the Signe ascending and the Lord thereof; and indeed in his person he was Saturnine, and vitiated according to Cauda in the ascendant, in his stature, mind or understanding; that is, was a little deformed in body, and extream covetous in disposition, etc.

The Signe of the sixth and his Lord signifies the Dogge; so must they have done if it had been a Sheep or Sheep, Hogs, Conies, etc, or any small Cattle.

The Signe of Gemini is West and by South, the quarter of heaven is West; Mercury the significator of the Dog, is in Libra a Westerne Signe but Southerne quarter of heaven, tending to the West; the Moon is in Virgo, a South-west Signe, and verging to the Westerne angle: the strength of the testimonies examined, I found the plurality to signifie the West, and therefore I judged, that the Dog ought to be Westward from the place where the Owner lived, which was at Temple-barre, wherefore I judged that the Dog was about Long-acre, or upper part of Drury-lane: In regard that Mercury Significator of the Beast, was in a Signe of the same Triplicity that Gemini his Ascendant is, which signifies Longon, and did not apply to a trine of the Cusp of the sixth house, I judged the Dog was not out of the lines of Communication, but in the same quarter; of which I was more confirmed by Sun and Saturn their trine. The Signe wherein Mercury is in, is Libra, an ayery Signe, I judged the Dog was in some chamber or upper room, kept privately, or in great secrecy: because Moon was under the Beames of the Sun, and Mercury Moon and Sun were in the eight house, but because the Sun on Monday following did apply by trine dexter to Saturn Lord of the ascendant, and Moon to sextile of Mars, having exaltation in the ascendant; I intimated, that in my opinion he should have his Dog againe, or newes of his Dog or small Beast upon Monday following, or neer that time; which was true; for a Gentleman of the querent's acquaintance, sent home the Dog the very same day about ten in the morning, who by accident comming to see a Friend in Long-acre, found the Dog chained up under a table, and knowing the Dog to be the Querent's, sent him home, as abovesaid, to my very great credit.

(William Lilly, *Christian Astrology*, 1647)

Lilly was not a modest man. After this touching tale of the dog returned, we come to one of his most famous cases, in which this astrological Sherlock Holmes tracks down the criminal, solves the mystery, and rights all wrongs.

Fish Stolen

Living in the Country 1637 I had bought at London some Fish for my provision in Lent, it came down by the Barge at Walton, on Saturday the 10. of Febr. one of the Watermen, instead of bringing my Fish home, acquainted me, their warehouse was robbed last night, and my Fish stolen: I took the exact time when I first heard the report, and erected the Figure accordingly, endeavouring to give my selfe satisfaction what became of my goods, and, if possible, to recover part or all of them againe.

I first observed, there was no peregrine Planet in angle but Jupiter, whom I found upon the cusp of the seventh house, the thing I lost was Fish, therefore any Gentleman would scorne such a course Commodity; I considered the signification of Jupiter in Scorpio, a moyst Signe, and the Significator of my Goods, viz. Mercury that he was in Pisces, a moyst Signe, and that the Part of Fortune was in Cancer, a moyst Signe. Discretion, together with Art, assisted me to think he must be a man whose profession or calling was to live upon the Water, that had my Goods, and that they were in some moyst place, or in some low roome, because the Part of Fortune was in Cancer, and the Moon in Taurus, an earthly Sign.

I was confident I should heare of my Goods againe, because Mercury Lord of my house of Substance, was applyed unto by a sextile of Moon, who was Lady of my Part of Fortune; and yet without hopes of recovering them, because Mercury Lord of my second, was in his fall and detriment, but as he was in his own Termes, and had a trine aspect to the Part of Fortune, there was hopes of some of my Goods.

There being never a Waterman in that Town of Walton neer unto the description of Jupiter in Scorpio, I examined what Fisherman there was of that complexion; and because Mars Lord of the 7th was departing the Sign Scorpio, viz. his owne and entring another Signe, I examined if never a Fisherman of Mars and Jupiter his nature had lately sold any Land, or was leaving his proper house, and going to another habitation; such a one I discovered, and that he was much suspected of theevery, who was a good fellow, lived neer the Thames side, and was a meer Fisherman . . .

The man that was the Thiefe was a Fisherman, of good stature, thick and fullbodied, faire of complexion, a red or yellowish haire.

I procured a Warrant from a Justice of peace, and reserved it privately until Sunday the eighteenth of February following, and then with a Constable and the Barge-man, I searched only that one house of this Fisherman suspected; I found part of my Fish in water, part eaten, part not consumed, all confessed.

(William Lilly, *Christian Astrology*, 1647)

The thrill of the chase seems to have been Lilly's chief interest in the affair, for he "freely remitted" what was left of his supply of fish, although he seems to have been a little put out that the "Portugal Onions" which had been stolen by mistake along with the fish had been cooked by the fisherman's wife. "I as heavily complained to the woman for seven Portugall Onyons which I lost; she not knowing what they were, made potage with them, as she said."

These cases have been set out at length because they provide some of the finest examples of precise, well-crafted divination readings that we can ever hope to meet. The answers fully meet the demands of the questions posed. Lilly's judgements grow from his technical skill, the imagination with which he applies it, and his ability to read a whole story from a horoscope. The quotations also help to show just how highly-developed certain systems of divination are, suggesting years of study and practice to develop facility with them.

Effective divination can also involve answers at the other end of the spectrum – brief, enigmatic, even ambiguous. Such were the pronouncements made at the ancient oracle of Delphi, in Greece. Indeed, it was said: "The Delphic oracle does not speak out; it does not hide: it signifies" (Heraclitus). This site was considered sacred, a centre of the earth, where the power of the gods might be tapped more readily. Its origins as a place of oracles stretch far back in time, well before 1000 BC, and it was originally consecrated to the earth goddess, Ge. Later, it was said that Apollo had taken over dominion of the site, and that the Delphic oracles were inspired by the exhalations, or "pneuma", that drifted up through a rift in the earth. The "Pythia", or presiding priestess, sat on a tripod above this chasm, and was considered to be a medium for the voice of Apollo. It is thought that a priest acted as an interpreter, putting her ecstatic answers into a comprehensible form.

Pythia's visitors were always male, and they were allowed to ask one question of her at a time, under strict ritual conditions. In the earlier years, as with astrology, these questions tended to be of national significance, later developing to deal with personal issues concerning Greek anxieties about marriages, voyages, loans and runaway slaves. A certain number of records of these questions and answers remain, although the oracles were considered such a natural part of Greek life that much of the procedure involved was never noted since it was common knowledge. The most striking answers, from our point of view, are those where the meaning does not lie simply in the most obvious interpretation of Pythia's utterances, but at another level, which may only be made apparent by the course of events. Two examples will show this clearly.

The first concerns Philip of Macedon, whom the priestess warned to guard himself against death coming from a chariot. Philip, quite naturally, got rid of all chariots from the land, but was killed in a duel, by a sword with a chariot motif on its hilt. Secondly, there is the tale of a philosopher who had lost the ability to laugh. He consulted the Pythia to ask how he might regain it, and was told: "Mother will give it to you at home." He went back to his mother, but to no avail – he could not laugh. Later, however, he visited the temple of Leto at Delos, Leto being the mother of Apollo. Leto's image in the temple was such an ugly, absurd lump that the afflicted philosopher burst out laughing and was cured.

These anecdotes are stories in their own right; one can imagine them as successful episodes in a play or book. Indeed, there is a strong similarity between these and the tale of Macbeth, who was told that no man born of woman would ever slay him, but was conquered by Duncan, who was "from his mother's womb/Untimely ripp'd". We cannot know, of course, how some of these more striking Delphic tales may have been embellished over the years, but what we read here is very much in keeping with the general tone of the priestesses' pronouncements, and with other examples of divination working itself out accurately in unexpected ways. The indication is that answers gained through divination stem from a different level of meaning, where the power of an image is being tapped rather than deriving from the usual chain of cause and effect. Such pronouncements also throw out interesting questions regarding the nature of fate; it could be argued that if Philip was fatally attracted to death through a chariot, then his destiny would still work itself out even when all the chariots were banished, and so he met his end through the image of a chariot. It could also be said that if he had penetrated to the heart of the meaning of the oracle, perhaps he would have had some chance to change that fate. In other words, he looked upon his life only as a progression of superficially linked events, and assumed that by getting rid of an overt threat he could avoid danger. If he had seen that the real danger came from a connection in his own fate between a chariot and death, and that the potency of that image would be enough to overthrow him, then he might have had the chance to break the connection and change the course of his life. Thus the Delphic oracle – signifying, not speaking nor hiding – may point to inner knowledge as the pathway to the future; through understanding, man may overthrow the chain of inevitability, which he in fact has created. Philip, after all, was warned, not condemned.

Thus it can be seen that divination may contain a potent ambiguity, an uncertainty that is not indecision, but an indication. Records do in fact show that questions asked of the Delphic oracles were based on the approach: "Would it be better if I did this?. . . . What is the likely outcome if I follow that path?" rather than on asking what the future held. Certain types of divination thrust the choice firmly back into our own hands, helping us to gain insight into the way events are likely to unfold, so that we may follow a particular thread or disentangle ourselves from it as appropriate.

The perils of misunderstanding the answers of divination, and the moral dangers of approaching it lightly, are amusingly set out in an Elizabethan woodcut, with accompanying text, in Geoffrey Whitney's *A Choice of Emblems* (1586). Three women are shown sitting at a table rolling dice, and the poem below reads:

Three carelesse dames, amongste their wanton toies,
Did throwe the dice, who firste of them shoulde die:
And shee that loste, did laughe with inwarde ioyes,
For that, shee thoughte her terme shoulde longer bee:
But loe, a tyle uppon her head did fall,
That deathe, with speede, this dame from dice did cal.

Even so, it falles, while carelesse times wee spende:
That evell happes, unlooked for doe comme.
But if wee hope, that GOD some good wil sende,
In earnest praier, then must wee not bee domme:

For blessinges good, come seild before our praier,
But evell thinges doe come before we feare.

The message of this little tale is all too clear, and, though the advice is rather prim, it does certainly indicate that it is not a good idea to fool around with questions of life and death.

The diviner who is consulted by someone with a serious question certainly has a responsibility. And the only way to act in the querent's interests is to go for the truth of the reading, even if it runs contrary to hopes or expectations. If a question is such that the diviner would not dare to pronounce the judgement if it proved unfavourable, then that question is better left alone. One's intentions are usually (I would like to say always!) to be helpful to the other person, but it is never helpful to mould the interpretation to suit his or her wishes. In my own experience as an astrologer, I learnt a valuable lesson from reading a friend's horoscope. The chart showed planetary configurations which were an unmistakeable sign of violence in the character, but to my knowledge she was such an easy-going type that I could not believe the evidence in front of me, and passed it over. A few weeks later, she mentioned to me casually that she had given a man she knew a black eye when he refused to do what she wanted! I realised that my duty as an astrologer was to be true to the horoscope as I understood it, not to bend it to what I thought would fit the person's character. Finding a way of presenting difficult truths is another matter, for the diviner's task is to be constructive. Questions and answers are the backbone of divination, the axis around which each interpretation revolves. The diviner himself acts as a messenger, posing the question, receiving and interpreting the answer, and communicating it to the querent.

Chapter 5

Approaching Divination

The person who practises divination faces many challenges beyond those of mastering the language and techniques. Divination demands commitment, discrimination and impartial but compassionate interpretation. Since few of us can make claims to such a superhuman standard of virtue, divination practice has built in many customs designed to give us the best chances of drawing on the wisdom that is available to us, and, perhaps, upon resources of knowledge that are not usually at our disposal.

Even the most trivial of divination practices tend to have their own rituals, while many of the major systems are steeped in ceremony. In terms of the image presented in Chapter 1, the purpose of such rituals is to direct attention to the door of the castle, away from the distractions of the garden, and to place the key in the lock of the door with precision. Of course, like all such practices, divination rituals can easily become rigid superstitions, their original purpose forgotten. It is all too common to cling to a particular custom as a talisman, and forget that it was intended as a means to an end. Rules need to be flexible, for under conditions where the usual procedures are wholly or partially inappropriate, the ingenious diviner can then devise others more suited to the case. If he or she understands the principles on which the practice is founded, then other ways of applying them can always be constructed.

A diviner needs discipline, but this is not the discipline of unvarying rules. As Derek Appleby remarks in *Horary Astrology*:

> Aside from the basic rules, the various guidelines set out by Lilly and other astrologers for the judgement of various types of question are merely the experience of that astrologer. It is a grave mistake to take the

view that if Lilly or someone else did not mention or sanction something it is not valid. The experience of other astrologers cannot be given the sanctity of firm rules. Every new moment of time is unique and is reflected in the heavens by a unique planetary pattern. That pattern must be interpreted anew by the individual astrologer and related to the matter under consideration.

(Derek Appleby, *Horary Astrology*, Aquarian Press, 1985)

With this advice in mind, we can turn to survey some of the customs that surround divination, and assess what their purpose may be.

Timing

Setting a time for embarking on a divinatory reading has always been considered important. This is usually done either by regulating the times at which questions may be asked, or by detecting from the reading itself that the time is not favourable for finding an answer. In the latter case, as we have already seen, a horary astrological chart may reveal that it is "too early" or "too late" to say what will come of the matter in question. It is often thought, too, by both natal and horary astrologers, that when Mercury, planet of calculations and communications, is in retrograde motion, the time is difficult for the judgement of charts. Mercury's backward movement (as seen from earth) may predispose the astrologer to mistakes and unsound interpretation.

This leads to the idea of regulated cycles, marking out the times at which divination may or may not take place. Some of these cycles seem to take their cue from natural timings, such as the seasons, the menstrual cycle in women, the phases of the moon, and so on, whereas others are more obviously man-made. The Delphic priestesses received their suppliants on only one day of every month, and closed down altogether for three months in winter. In British folk traditions, certain forms of divination were attached to particular times of the year, such as Hallowe'en, New Year, Midsummer's Eve and Easter. While some of these are related to significant points in the earth's orbit, such as the equinox or solstice, others are tied into religious or social observances. "Care Sunday", for instance, the fifth in Lent, was the traditional time in Northumberland to practise marriage divination with a dish of peas. During the family meal "each person helped himself in turn from the dish until only a few peas were left, and these were taken one by one. Whoever got the last pea would be the first to marry. Another method was to hide a bean among the peas; the person who found it in his or her helping was the lucky individual." (Christina Hole, *A Dictionary of British Folk Customs*, Hutchinson, 1976).

A great deal of time could be spent, and perhaps wasted, deliberating whether the selected times for divination coincide with any objectively or naturally favourable moments for plundering the treasure-houses of hidden knowledge. Perhaps it is more helpful to consider the fact that human life has an ebb and flow which needs to be reflected in divination. Using those well-known words from Ecclesiastes:

> To everything there is a season, and a time to every purpose under the heaven.
>
> A time to be born, and a time to die; a time to plant and a time to pluck up that which is planted.
>
> A time to kill, and a time to heal; a time to break down, and a time to build up;
>
> A time to weep, and a time to laugh; a time to mourn, and a time to dance;
>
> A time to cast away stones, and a time to gather stones together; a time to embrace, and a time to refrain from embracing;
>
> A time to get, and a time to lose; a time to keep, and a time to cast away;
>
> A time to rend, and a time to sew; a time to keep silence, and a time to speak;
>
> A time to love, and a time to hate; a time of war and a time of peace. (Chapter 3, verses 1–8)

Social customs and religious observances help to regulate the cycle of life. We are affected by several different cycles – our bodily rhythms, seasonal cycles, planetary patterns and plenty more which scientists and occultists alike delight in discovering. To set up a particular cycle of action and restraint is to impose order on these fluctuating energy patterns. Such a cycle may have its foundation in a natural or celestial cycle rather than a cultural one – the Anglo-Saxons, for instance, paid particular attention to the moon's phases, and singled out two days of every month which they considered unfavourable for new beginnings. But whatever the basis, setting up a structure of timing can help to draw our abilities into a recognisable and predictable pattern, which we can then use constructively. The process is somewhat similar to that of conditioning the routine of a baby, who is gradually taken from a totally instinctive, and rather chaotic, pattern of feeding and sleeping into one that fits the generally acceptable timings of meals and of day- and night-time activity, as perceived by the parents or society as a whole.

We have the ability to create cycles to channel certain functions and processes. Contrary to what is sometimes suggested, it is impossible to go with our natural rhythms entirely, because we are affected by many different rhythms whose high and low points do not necessarily coincide. We can therefore select one main rhythm, giving it emphasis and perhaps ritual significance, and exploiting its inherent potential. Even in the simple, and perhaps naive, practice of divining through the dish of peas, it can be seen that to carry this out every day would make a nonsense of it. Reserving it for one special day of the year, however, will at the very least generate attention, interest and concentration, the conditions under which divination flourishes.

As I have stressed before, divination does not produce consistent results. Therefore, it may often be best to reserve readings for the most propitious moments. These may simply be when the diviner feels at his or her best, but as this can be a hit-or-miss affair, it is often more effective to tie divination into specific timings stemming from an accepted cycle of energy peaks and troughs. If such a cycle is kept by a group or community of people, then it is likely to generate a more accessible rhythm which the diviner can use. Just on a social level, for instance, it is difficult in England to ignore the excitement at the approach of Christmas, a marking point in nearly everyone's year. The diviner who wishes to work to maximum effect may choose to restrict readings to times which have more potency as defined in individual, community or religious terms.

Ceremonies

Other rituals surrounding divination also highlight the deliberate setting of intention. The Delphic oracle is the classic example of this. When fully developed, it was contained in a specially consecrated temple, enclosing an inner sanctuary in which the Pythia made her pronouncements. As the cult grew, so the rituals became more significant. The enquirer had to prove his seriousness by making offerings on approaching the temple; a sacred cake might be dedicated on the altar outside, or sheep or goats sacrificed. The sacrifice itself was considered highly significant, for if the goat trembled then the spirit of Apollo was close at hand. It was not unknown for the priests to pour cold water on the hapless beast to achieve the desired effect. Only male visitors to the temple were allowed, and they were instructed to "think pure thoughts and speak well-omened words" before putting their questions to the oracle.

The Pythia herself, on the appropriate day of the month for taking up her oracular duties, would take a ceremonial bath after dawn and be fumigated with laurel leaves and barley meal. Everything that happened in the temple was governed by a strict code of practice, designed to provide the best conditions for invoking the spirit of Apollo to give counsel. On the fire in the temple only pine and laurel were burnt, as these were woods which had special affinity with the deity.

Such rituals, intended to simplify and to focus energies, could often become over-complex and, indeed, even bureaucratic. Certain of the Greek oracles became so popular, and their visitors so importunate, that a whole battery of rules and regulations had to be introduced to cope with the influx. These are some of the instructions preserved at the oracle of Apollo of Corope:

The commanders and the guardians of the law must enroll staff-bearers from among the citizens, namely, three men under thirty who shall have the authority to punish unruly elements. If one of the enrolled fails to show up, he shall pay a fine of fifty drachmas to the city. . . . When those mentioned above are present at the oracle, and perform the sacrifice according to tradition, with a favourable result, the secretary of the god shall collect, immediately after the sacrifice, the petitions of those who wish to consult the oracle, write all their names on a white tablet, and exhibit the white tablet at once in front of the temple and lead them in, calling them up according to the order of their names, unless someone may have the privilege of being called ahead of the others. . . . In the sanctuary, the persons entered on the lists shall sit properly, in shining [i.e. festive] garments, crowned with laurel wreaths, clean and sober, and they shall receive the tablets from those who deliver the oracle.

(Quoted in *Arcana Mundi*, ed. Georg Luck, Johns Hopkins University Press, 1985)

Rarely do we have to go to such lengths today to consult Madam Rosa, Reader of Fortune and Destiny, at the local fun fair. But even she is usually seated in a tent or a caravan, an inner sanctum into which one must pass to be initiated into the mysteries of one's destiny. Making a space in which divination can take place, whether it be mental or physical, seems to be a feature common to diviners of many types and dispositions.

Often diviners of the priestess or shamanic type were expected to submit themselves completely to the ritualistic structure of their practice, leaving behind any claims to a private life. Through doing this, it was maintained, an innate aptitude for divining could be brought to full power, even in those with very little experience or education.

A Pythia might be a very ordinary woman, possessed of no knowledge worth reckoning. It was only when under Apollo's immediate influence that she saw all time and all space as one.

(H. W. Parker, *The Delphic Oracle*, Blackwell, 1956)

An Open Mind – Innocence and Psychism

Plainly, divination cannot be practised without a certain receptivity, a readiness to let go of normal logic and be open to intuition and imagination. In the present social climate this is often considered woolly-minded, even dangerous, because for a century or so the scientific and rational approach has been thought to have greatest validity. An unfortunate polarisation has occurred between intellect and imagination; now, hopefully, they are beginning to be reconciled, for science cannot flourish without imagination, and divination, as I hope this book will show, needs thought and reason in its structure.

The willingness to reverse the normal priorities, and to allow intuition the space in which to work, seems to have been shown by rather more women than men at the current time. In general, the female interest in astrology, Tarot cards and so on is stronger than the masculine. Possibly the psychic and imaginative faculties are closer to the surface in women, and less easily suppressed.

In children, too, there is a readiness to accept new impressions without automatically discounting those that do not fit into the usual rational patterns. Children are naturally inclined to divination. When Iona and Peter Opie collected all the examples of juvenile magical and divinatory practices that they could find for their book *The Lore and Language of Schoolchildren* (Oxford University Press, 1959), they pointed out the ambiguous attitude of their informants:

> Many charms and rites are of course practised by children 'just for fun', because everybody else practises them, and it is the fashion. Other charms, although recognized as being 'probably silly', are repeated because they also feel that there 'may be something in it'. Others, again, are practised because it is in the nature of children to be attracted by the mysterious: they appear to have an innate awareness that there is more to the ordering of fate than appears on the surface.

Different authorities might round out this statement by adding that children have fewer pre-conceptions of what is and what is not possible, and that they are therefore more open to experiencing changed orders of time and space. Many parents, myself included, have observed also that young children can be extraordinarily telepathic, and are on occasion able to describe something that is happening out of sight, an ability that usually recedes later. A teacher of meditation once remarked that children are often seen to pause and go into a complete state of meditation (and this does not mean day-dreaming) but that they are never aware that they are doing this. Here, I think, lies the essential difference between children's natural capabilities and those which adults cultivate deliberately. Children often do not know what they know, are incapable of bringing out insights to order, and do not recognize the difference between levels of experience. Sometimes certain cultures will single out particularly gifted children for training, as is the case in the Tibetan monasteries. England has its own traditions, too. In West Somerset there is the example of the Chime Child, which Ruth Tongue, the folklorist and herself a Chime Child, describes:

> They must be born between midnight on a Friday and cock-crow on a Saturday, as I am told I was – both these days being regarded as full of unseen danger among some villagers. This was all explained to me before I was five . . .
>
> 'They that be born of a Friday's chime
> Be masters of musick and finders of rhyme,
> And every beast will do what they say,
> And every herb that do grow in the clay,
> They do see what they see and they hear what they hear,
> But they never do tell in a hundred year.'
>
> (Ruth Tongue, *The Chime Child*, Routledge and Kegan Paul, 1967)

Developing a child's natural inclination or ability to divine, however, is fraught with danger. Children need to be secure in the mundane, everyday world, and to distinguish the normal perameters of experience. Although children have been used as diviners – and used is the right word – it is hardly to be recommended as a practice. Possibly in cases where such a practice is accompanied by a well-structured religious training it can be justified, but where a child is asked to use these abilities for adult purposes, the danger of creating psychological instability is surely too great.

The fully-fledged adult psychic, too, may have trouble maintaining a normal, stable existence if he or she is open to impressions and energies from beyond the personal sphere for too much of the time. Divination and psychism are not the same, as I have already pointed out in Chapter 1. But psychism cannot be left out completely from the discussion of divination and the human abilities that go with it. Most diviners, after all, have a degree of intuitive ability, which they choose to direct through a divinatory system. And yet it is also possible to practise divination without any conscious awareness of psychic abilities, especially where the techniques are complex and mastering them requires a great deal of mental effort. The word "psychic" is a loaded one; it can describe simply the ability to pick up on the thoughts and impressions already in the mind of the client and feed them back. "Psychic" abilities may certainly be an aid to the diviner in drawing out certain unseen elements and possibilities from the atmosphere and easing the way to divination, but psychic and divinatory powers do not seem to be identical. However, to provide a complete model delineating the difference between the two would require much discussion and questioning, well beyond the scope of this book.

Attitudes and Choices in the Practice of Divination

I shall now pick up some of the points introduced in the last chapter and amplify them, setting them in the context of the personal practice of divination. As already mentioned, choosing an appropriate divination system can be an important matter. Someone interested in taking up a method of divination needs to consider his or her own disposition, as well as the materials and instruction available. A divination system represents the doorway from one world to another. Therefore it should have the quality of leading us forward, encouraging speculation, stimulating our curiosity. It is not to be expected that an individual will find all systems equally enticing. The numerologist and the Tarot card reader may be quite divergent in their outlook, the former enjoying the play of ideas that underlies the principle of number, the latter finding the power of vision aroused by pictorial symbols. The Tarot reader may feel that numerology is artificial, and the numerologist that the Tarot cards are too fluid. This is only an example; we are by no means restricted to mastering only one system, and may find that eventually coming to learn three or four systems helps to express different facets of our ability and personality.

The decision to practise divination is, in any case, rarely taken at an intellectual level. Often the interest stretches right back to the early years of life. The actual decision to take up the practice may then be triggered off, years later, by experiencing a divination reading at first hand. Although divination can be learnt from books – the techniques at least – there is usually an initiation into the process through personal contact. It is similar to the difference between learning all about birds through natural history books and seeing them live. The reference books are very helpful, and can continue to be useful for identification purposes, but their two-dimensional representation of a particular species is never quite the same as its living counterpart. The essence of divination can come across through practice in a way that cannot be conveyed by printed words. A great deal is made of the passing on of knowledge, initiation into secret traditions and so on, but what is really important is to come into contact with the life of a tradition at first hand. It then has a chance to be absorbed into one's consciousness and stimulate imagination and speculation from a basis of experience. Once a person has gained facility with a divination system, and has a sense of its purpose, then it is quite possible to try out other practices from books, or other cultures, or even to invent systems. But, to start with, the threshold is only likely to be crossed by taking up a system in which one can have a certain amount of personal instruction.

Looking at the question of choice in divination from a different angle, we have seen that an appropriate system must be chosen for a particular question: palmistry would be no help in finding a lost necklace, and character reading would not be the province of the dowser. The language of the system must have the kind of vocabulary that can actually answer the question posed. It is useful to make a distinction between systems which can give fairly cut-and-dried answers, such as dowsing and horary astrology, and those which help to build up a whole picture, such as natal astrology and Tarot cards. Likewise, it is as well to assess which particular area of hidden knowledge a system is particularly designed to penetrate. If indications about future events are required then one would choose palmistry rather than psychometry which deals mainly with the past. The practitioner must weigh up his or her own aptitude, the environment worked in and the type of question posed, to decide which divination system to employ.

Approaching each individual operation of divination also needs care and attention. Earlier in the chapter I showed how traditional ritual practices have built up around divination to clear the way and safeguard the passage. Such rituals can be translated into mental preparation which the careful diviner will always go through, even if he or she does very little in the way of outward ceremony. A diviner always has the choice of accepting a question or refusing it – unless he is in the clutches of a tyrant, as Joseph was in the Bible story! He needs to be convinced that both he and the querent are willing to listen to whatever information the operation throws up. It is natural for hopes and wishes to be involved, but there should also be the space for receiving other indications apart from those which are most desired. Many a request for divination conceals an attempt to force the issue. This is especially relevant when an individual is his or her own diviner, for then there is no other person to check up on intention and an honest scrutiny of one's own motivations is necessary.

It may also be unwise in many cases to accept questions which are put from a cynical standpoint, just to test out whether divination really works. This does not mean that a healthy scepticism should be frowned upon, and only "believers" allowed to ask questions. It has more to do with the spirit in which the question is put; if it is one of honest enquiry, then the divination is more likely to be effective. Of course, the diviner may decide to do battle in the manner of the old magicians and take on a sneering opponent to prove the power of his art! But it is as well to recognize that this is a risky venture; the diviner needs to be secure enough to accept possible loss of face, or else the tendency arises to want to go on and on trying to prove to a hostile world that there is some truth in divination.

There are also important ethical considerations in any process of divination. As suggested earlier, the diviner needs to be happy that the question is an appropriate one, and that he or she is not prying into a third party's business in which there is no right to meddle. It is also useful to know – though not always easy to ascertain – that the outcome of a divination reading will not be used as a weapon against another person. This can be especially relevant where the question concerns relationships, divorce, etc. It all ties into the key idea that divination is open-ended, requiring detached application and a receptive frame of mind. If either party is strongly inclined to manipulate the situation, then the reading may be faulty and the transaction corrupted.

A diviner may have to clear his or her personal space, too, in order to gain the degree of detachment needed to operate the system. It is often thought that to enter into divination full of sympathy, righteous indignation, enthusiasm or other feeling is an inspired approach, but, in fact, prevailing emotions can cloud the issue and detract from the fullness of the reading. The sphere of operation in which divination takes place is a sensitive one, and clarity of intention is needed to direct the reading beyond the immediate present. The diviner with psychic leanings or strong emotional sympathies needs to let go of all the information that is coming in from immediate impressions. This can be a hard discipline, but if it is not attempted, then all the diviner will be doing is feeding back to the questioner his or her current preoccupations. It can be helpful to make sure that the question is clearly formulated, that the querent knows precisely what it is, even if he or she does not speak it aloud.

Every diviner will find the best personal way of proceeding with a reading. This may involve taking quite a long time about it, or leaving a gap between the request for divination and actually embarking on the reading. A shift must be made from the usual revolutions of the mental wheels to the alert and receptive clarity that is needed. A diviner must feel free to pursue the reading as he or she feels is appropriate; it is common for the querent to want the whole process on his own terms, and to try to insist on particular answers or explanations at inappropriate moments. This throws open some awkward issues, especially if the diviner is charging for the reading, since pressure can be applied by the client to get his money's worth in the way he wants it. This is one of the reasons why a large number of diviners do not charge for their services, since this leaves them completely free to set their own terms and code of practice.

Traditionally, the diviner has never been at the beck and call of the client, except in the cases of employment by potentates, and even here certain seers have gone to their death rather than deviate from what they have considered to be the truth of a reading.

Motivation

It is not especially helpful for the diviner to be locked into constant self-analysis, but it *is* useful to keep a weather-eye on one's motivations for wishing to practise divination. We are attracted to divination in the first place for something that it seems to promise, and this alluring aspect will colour our approach, the type of questions we attract, and the results that transpire.

From the image of the castle described in the opening chapter, it can be seen that divination may help to give a sense of purpose to life. It reveals underlying patterns, gives meaning to apparently trivial or random phenomena, and adds an exciting dimension to the humdrum plane of daily life. The diviner who senses this strongly may indeed be able to transform the quality of his own life, and cast light upon other people's, inspiring them, too, with purpose. The search for meaning, however, like all motivations, has its difficulties. The diviner may feel impelled to bring a strong sense of meaning out of every reading, and feel cheated if this does not happen. I have been at some pains to show that divination is not a factory set-up, working on automatic production. Many elements, both within and outside the diviner's control, may prevent a reading from being fully effective. In the performing arts, musicians, actors and the like have to learn to live with the fact that they cannot be at their best all the time. They endeavour to work consistently, but their own physical and mental state, the attitude of the audience, the environment, even the mood of the day itself are all variable factors which will affect the performance. Through technique and dedicated application, many difficulties can be overcome, but the best will in the world cannot guarantee perfect results. The real challenge then is to be able to accept the validity of those peak performances – or divination readings – without dismissing them as lucky chance simply because there were others which were not so good.

Allied to the quest for meaning is that for hidden knowledge. Here divination can promise much – discovery of hidden substances, knowledge of character, of future events, of significant potential. A key to knowledge is, after all, what many people dedicate their lives to finding. Here again the practitioner of divination has to guard against too strong expectations of success. He or she also needs to keep a philosophical attitude towards the kind of knowledge gained through the reading, for the type of reality revealed through divination has a habit of shedding layer after layer like an onion! It is also tempered by the state of being of the diviner, and by the point in time at which the querent stands. Often an astrologer, for instance, finds that a client turns up with a problem or with a horoscope that relates strongly to the astrologer's own life at that time, and that the so-called "answers" which arise are relevant to both parties. And now here the astrologer, or diviner, must be open-minded enough to accept that this knowledge is useful and genuine, even if it does not fit the normal criterion of objectivity. As long as the astrologer can retain the objectivity to recognise that the chart is *not* his own, the problem not *exactly* identical to his, then the reading can flower, for it is stemming from a sympathetic resonance between the states of astrologer and client but is not restricted by this. Knowledge comes through divination, but not always in the terms we expect.

The third common category of motivation is the desire to help others. At first glance this seems simple enough, but in fact it can be the most complex and difficult of all. We have already seen how the urge to sympathise can in fact get in the way of divination if it is not superseded by a clearer and more detached attitude. There are also the problems that may arise of wanting to heal and help others in the hope of healing oneself, of wanting to gain a superior position by being able to show others the way, or of trying to serve a very personal idea of justice. I would say here that there is no such thing as the perfect and pure desire to help others, and that for all of us, when we wish to help, certain elements of these desires creep in. The important step to take is to recognise that they may exist, and, rather than fight them, just observe them and grant them no great significance in the reading that is about to take place. They only turn into a real threat when either they work away unnoticed, or are given too much prominence as something we have to fight against – in which case they are likely to turn into fierce opponents.

A further difficulty which may arise from our wish to help others is that we take all their problems upon ourselves. To work divination effectively, it is necessary to be as unburdened as possible. There is not much room in that doorway into the castle to bring in luggage! People may often consult a diviner because they are under great emotional pressure, and may see a reading as an opportunity to unload all their agitated feelings and fears. This is not the primary function of divination, and the diviner needs to keep clearly in mind the distinction between divination and therapy, or healing. The therapist acquires different skills to bring out the client's powerful feelings and drives, and to handle these in an appropriate manner. The diviner who tries to act as therapist as well – especially without the proper training – may find that he or she becomes a target for the client's problems. It is easy for a naturally sympathetic person to be affected by the states of others, and to have his or her own effectiveness diminished as a result. The wise diviner encourages a state of clarity in the questioner, as well as in himself. This enables both to get out of the powerful web of normal consciousness, and tap into an expansive world of knowledge. This is the true help that divination can offer. The diviner is a guide, not a doctor; he leads the expedition, and interprets the landmarks.

Finally, in this chapter on approaches to divination, we come to the question of finishing off a reading. The best principle to follow here is simply that – finish it off! The journey is ended, and the diviner and querent part company, metaphorically at least. It is often helpful for the diviner to allow some time for other questions to be put that are relevant to the reading, and then to indicate clearly that it is at an end. Thus the session can be grounded; the results do not need to be picked over again and again.

Chapter 6

Creating Systems

Many divination systems that have come down to us are hundreds, if not thousands of years old. Throughout the centuries they may evolve and diversify, adapting to different cultural settings and contemporary needs. It is easy to assume that an effective divination method must have the sanctity of age. But all systems have to start somewhere, and there is no reason why equally interesting divination practices should not be created in our own day, too. In this chapter, therefore, the key elements that go into a system are considered, followed by a brief look at some methods of divination that have been initiated in recent years.

Divination – a Microcosmos

An effective form of divination is like a small world, a microcosmos. This world in miniature becomes a sphere of activity which may be observed, and in which parallels may be found with the patterns of human life. It is to some extent like the sealed vessel of the alchemists. The vessel, with the chosen substances placed inside, was placed over the fire and carefully watched by the alchemist. The whole process of change that took place within the vessel – the appearance of different colours, of vapours and so on – was seen as corresponding to the state of the alchemist himself, and to the very principles of creation. As one alchemical writer claimed, the vessel could become the medium through which he could witness the making of the world, the coming of the Egyptian darkness described in the Bible, and the appearance of glorified bodies at the resurrection.

For the diviner, the microcosm of the method used is such that questions can be posed and a response to them appear through the chosen medium. The microcosm can be the world of Nature, a set of cards, a family of planets, or anything which has a unity whose parts are capable of differing combinations or movements. A bowl of goldfish – a more prosaic image after the alchemist's vessel – provides a good basic picture for this. The world of the fish is enclosed and its boundaries can be seen, but at any moment in time it will present a different picture, as there is an almost limitless variety of ways in which the fish can swim in relation to each other.

I do not wish to labour this image too much, for it serves as a fundamental concept, and different practices of divination will have a varying emphasis. They may use a "static"or a "moving" picture, extract a partial image from the sphere, or try to encompass the whole. Looking at different systems mentioned in previous chapters will help to illustrate this point. The idea to bring forward here is that when a divination system is created, it must define its sphere of operation – it has to have a wholeness from which its parts derive, rather than the other way round.

How are the enclosed worlds of divination chosen, and how are their limits set? Let us return to astrology to provide an example for this. Astrology takes the unit of the solar system as its world. The centre of this sphere is the earth; astrology is earth-based, as it plots the movements of sun, moon and planets as they appear to man on earth. In astrology, the fixed stars, that is, distant galaxies, are taken as the ultimate band encircling this sphere, without depth in space as far as life on earth is concerned. This is the unity that is defined in astrology, and the activity within it is described in terms of its moving parts, especially in their relationship to the ecliptic, that outer band which is an extension of the solar system plane to the galactic. This plane of the ecliptic is in fact the circle of the zodiac. The moving parts, the planets, sun and moon, are also plotted in their relationship to each other and to the fixed central point of the sphere, the earth.

We know, of course, that the earth does move, and it is the sun which is at the centre of the solar system. We also know that this system is just one insignificant grouping among an infinity of suns and galaxies. From the human point of view, while man remains an earth-centred creature, this makes no difference. The astrological map relates directly to our experience of life and our perceptions of our spatial position. Astronomically, too, a horoscope is a perfectly correct map of the solar system as viewed from earth.

The world of astrology is thus defined spatially, and space is the medium in which the planets move, rather as the goldfish swim through the water in their bowl. We have seen earlier, too, how divining from the flight of birds uses a spatial sphere, sometimes called "the temple". In palmistry the microcosm to be considered is the hand of the individual, representing character and destiny. In astrology, the world defined is one far greater in scale than man himself, and the principle applied is that by studying this sphere which is larger in dimension, one may come to understand the smaller, human sphere. Palmistry works the other way round, for the smaller unit of the hand is said to embody all the characteristics of the complete being. Nice points of philosophy arise here, however, for the notions of greater and lesser can be interchangeable to some extent; if we say that man contains the elements of all life within him, including the world of sun, moon and stars, this immediately shifts the perspective, and perhaps suggests that physical and mental scale are not the same thing.

Numerical Structure

Once the unity of a divination method has been determined, in nearly every case number is used to help define its basic structure. As discussed earlier, a twofold ordering underlies several systems. This division of a world into yes and no, black and white, affirmation and denial, gives us at once a vocabulary for distinguishing a whole variety of human perceptions and experiences. To clarify this idea that numbering defines the quality of a system, I should like to quote from an article written for *The Astrological Journal* ("Cabbala, Numbers and Aspects", Cherry Gilchrist, Vol XXIV no 1 Winter 1981–2):

Number symbolism can be very difficult. The student searching to discover the inherent meaning of each number may become confused and discouraged at the mass of varying symbols and interpretations that he encounters. Frequently, different systems of mathematics, geometry, philosophy, religion, music and magic will offer quite different meanings for specific numbers, and it can become hard to give credence to any idea of objective number symbol at all.

I think one point that is often overlooked is that numbers are used within a specific context, and that the number series of the context makes a great difference to the interpretation. For instance, astrology is based primarily on the number twelve, the enneagram of Gurdjieff on nine, the Tarot pack on twenty-two, and the Western musical octave on eight. So that the numbers which denote wholeness and completion in each system will be twelve, nine, twenty-two and eight respectively. . . . Number is somewhat like language; there is a blueprint, or prototype of meaning which all might agree on, but a number, like a word, can be used with many shades of meaning depending upon the context, and may even, at times, be used in opposite ways. (Think of the word 'terrific'; dictionary definition is 'causing great terror', but it is used in popular speech to mean 'marvellous' or 'very impressive'.)

Number and wholeness are therefore linked in symbolic and creative systems. Even where a divination system is not founded on a spatial sphere, we can imagine its entirety as represented by a globe, a microcosm which we may want to describe by dividing it into different areas. A binary divination practice splits this globe into two equal halves, dark and light, left and right, receptive and creative. A system founded on the principle of three will usually be dynamic, concerned with the laws of interaction – the "eternal triangle" is a common theme in staged and domestic drama. A fourfold order may define different states of being, different areas of experience. It is often hierarchical, like the four elements, earth, water, fire and air, said to correspond to the physical, emotional, creative and spiritual levels in man. The elements have long been used to symbolise the qualities of man's faculties and to define the hierarchy of the visible world.

The higher numbers most commonly used in divination systems are six, seven, ten, twelve and twenty-two. Six can be interpreted as the process of creating a structure – as illustrated in the hexagrams of the I Ching, while seven is a scale or spectrum and is often shown as a hierarchy. The higher the number, the more likely that it will contain combinations of the properties of numbers. Twelve, for example, can be seen as the result of multiplying three by four. In astrology, the twelve signs of the zodiac represent the different types of human identity which result from mixing the three principles of energy interaction (cardinal – initiating, fixed – stabilising, and mutable – adapting) with the four elements. Each sign is thus a combination of one "triplicity" and one "quadruplicity". The opening sign of the zodiac, Aries, is designated as cardinal fire. The psychological type that Aries represents is built up from this picture of initiating enthusiasm that cardinality and fieriness suggest.

Twenty-two, the number of cards in the Major Arcana of the Tarot pack, may be seen as three sets of seven plus one over, "The Fool", signifying the beginning and the end, the card that lies beyond the others, the outside influence that can transform the existing patterns. Most divination systems are quite complex in their final form, and make use of more than one set of numerical properties. However, when examined closely, one fundamental concept of numbering is usually found from which further complexities and divisions are derived. Anyone creating a divination system, therefore, must decide upon the basic numbering which is to underly the system. Sometimes the "microcosm" itself will suggest a code of number. The human hand, for instance, has ten fingers; for observing movement in space, with birds and animals, there are four basic directions defined, extending to six when height and depth are added.

The Symbols Used

The world of divination must have content. It must have forms which can be described and discerned, which can combine in different ways, and to which meaning can be attributed. If the practice of divination is to engage the imagination at all, then these symbols will be more effective if they impress us at a level which is not purely intellectual. They need to have something of the archetypal within them, with an intrinsic meaning which can be understood in a variety of specific ways.

When symbols are discussed, the question often arises whether they have true universal significance, or purely a cultural meaning. Most long-standing divination systems are in fact based on principles which are common to all human life, but these are often clothed in a way which reflects the cultural or religious bias of the society in which the system originated. Such a bias need not prevent us appreciating a system which emerges from another culture or era, if its principles are still clearly defined. And a certain amount of "clothing" is usually necessary to give colour and form, to stir our imagination and speculative faculty. Each system has to have its own identity. One might find parallels of meaning, for instance, between a specific Tarot card, a rune, and a geomantic figure, but they are all individual in form and very obviously products of different systems.

The basic principles of a divination system may, I have suggested, be equated with archetypes. C. G. Jung, who made a particular study of the role of archetypes, was at pains to point out that an archetype is an abstraction, which can appear in many different guises:

> A primordial image is determined as to its content only when it has become conscious and is therefore filled out with the material of conscious experience. Its form, however ... might perhaps be compared to the axial system of a crystal, which, as it were, performs the crystalline structure in the mother liquid, although it has no material existence of its own. This first appears according to the specific way in which the ions and molecules aggregate. The archetype in itself is empty and purely formal, nothing but a *facultas praeformandi*, a possibility of representation which is given *a priori*.

(Quoted in the glossary of C. G. Jung, *Memories, Dreams, Reflections*, Collins and Routledge and Kegan Paul, 1963)

The complete approach to constructing a divination system would include the struggle to abstract archetypes and establish them as a complete unity. However, this is a task of great magnitude, and is not easily undertaken by individuals, relating more to evolving myths and perceptions of man and society. No one could have written all the basic Arthurian legends in a couple of weeks' solitude with quill and parchment, for instance. They are plainly connected to powerful, commonly-held ideals of chivalry, justice, spiritual quest, pure love and Christian endeavour. In a sense, the formulation of these myths was the apex of a pyramid, the encoding of concepts that had already been established. The major divination systems appear either to draw from existing mythology, or to evolve through the centuries. The Tarot, for instance, while bearing the marks of a system devised quite deliberately and probably in one go, still makes use of evocative symbols from the common store, such as Death the Reaper and the Wheel of Fortune. Astrology, on the other hand, took literally thousands of years to reach its basic formulation, and could be said to be evolving still. So the individual who aspires to create a divination system is likely to encapsulate some of the current symbolism available, and perhaps build on pre-existing systems.

The symbols used must be in keeping with one another, and are usually capable of being combined, giving rise to a wealth of specific interpretations. To illustrate this, let us take the simple example of a set of four symbols – the wand, knife, cup and disc. These, in fact, are the basis of the four suits of playing cards, as clubs, spades, hearts and diamonds respectively. They also appear in the Minor Arcana of the Tarot, and in other systems of working. Plainly, they have a universal application, for they are emblems of tools and forms used in just about every human society. They may acquire cultural meanings, too, when the cup becomes the Christian communion chalice and the stick an Amerindian totem pole. Added to this, the archetypes can take on qualities which reflect emotional and abstract principles. The cup, for instance, is a container which may be a source of refreshment if it is filled with water, of death if it contains poison. It can represent the storing of memories and impressions in the psyche; it can signify the human soul, ready to receive a measure of divine grace. The knife, on the other hand, is a tool for cutting and severing. It defines limits, breaks connections, implements decisions and cuts away corruption. The stick, or wand, marks direction, becomes the spindle of necessity and an emblem of human will, while the disc is the formation of a base, the foundation of movement, as in the wheel, and the symbol of constant energy, as in the disc of the sun.

The list could go on and on. Each person will see something a little different in these symbols, but the essential principles remain. They are therefore potentially a useful set of symbols for divination, for they have a core of meaning which gives rise to a great variety of specific connotations. This means that their potential "vocabulary" is wide, and capable of being applied to different types of questions.

The scope of interpretation extends still further when we start treating the symbols in combination, in the way that cards in the Tarot pack are combined in a lay-out and in the way that planets in a horoscope are considered in their relationship to one another. This can be perceived very easily on the physical level. A stick and knife combined, for instance, make a spear. A stick and a cup create a ladle. Add in a fifth symbol, a cord, as is common in magical practice; this, sometimes designated as the element of ether, is said to rule and bind the other four. Now the possibilities multiply fast. A cord and a stick make a whip, a cord and discs a necklace, and so on. Once again, these can be applied to human experience, for a whip suggests drive, energy and ruthlessness, while a necklace symbolises beauty and adornment. If we start taking sets of three symbols, different types of possibilities arise. We could say that a cup, cord and knife together represent a bond of love that is being severed. Or, if it is cup, cord and disc, an affection that is about to be given a firm basis, through the ceremony of marriage, for instance. The combination of symbols thus becomes a source of dynamic interaction, suggesting situations which arise and the activities which alter them.

Formulating a System

We have now arrived at the point where the general process of creating a divination system can be described. The sequence may not be the same in all cases, but the stages can be defined basically as:

1. Define the sphere which encompasses the system.
2. Discover, or deliberately set up, the numerical structure which is to underly it.

3. Create, or choose, a set of symbols for use. Give them a character which helps to define the individuality of the system.
4. Decide how the system is to operate. Will it involve shuffling cards, tossing pebbles, watching birds, etc? What is its code of practice? What kind of questions can it tackle, and when and how should these be asked?

Naturally, some of these stages of development may be implicit in the original inspiration. A system may be born complete in its essentials, but need working out as regards detail. If, finally, it seems to be lacking or unbalanced in some respect, then it can be helpful to think about each of the stages separately, and see whether each has been adequately embodied in the system.

The major question now remains: What does it all mean? How is a system to be assigned meaning? Hopefully, some of this will already have been made clear. The underlying numerical structure will give some skeletal meaning to the system at the very least, both from the fundamental implications of number and from the scale of number used. In astrology, for instance, the zodiac is twelvefold, and thus the signs Aries, Cancer, Libra and Capricorn, which are the first, fourth, seventh and tenth signs respectively, are coloured in their interpretation by their positions in the zodiac, since they represent the start of four different quarters in the circle. They form the axes of the zodiac, the initiating (Aries) and balancing (Libra) axis and the rooted, enclosed (Cancer) and the outward, external (Capricorn) axis. The circle of twelve gives a fundamental source of interpretation for the zodiac signs.

If spatial directions are used, then perhaps the relationship to the observer will help to define meaning. That which lies behind me has different connotations from that which is in front, and this notion can be extended to include significance in time – behind corresponding to past, and ahead to the future. Left and right likewise may be defined from our associations with these orientations, usually the intuitive, shadowy implications for the left and rational, bright connotations for the right. That which is above plainly differs from that which is below, the former often corresponding to aspirations, the spiritual and exalted, the latter to the practical, mundane and earthily energetic.

Just as the most elegant car has not proved its worth until it has motored off down the road, so the created divination system has to be tested out in practice to see if it can be effectively applied. Adjustments may need to be made before its final form is satisfactory. It is often better to go for a simpler approach if problems arise. Too many elaborate details can be confusing, whereas a simple, practical method can always be built upon over the course of time.

Modern Divination Systems

Every now and then, one comes across new divination systems. I shall mention three here, and then suggest the symbols for a fourth, with which readers might like to experiment. All three systems discussed borrow to a certain extent from other traditions; it is extremely hard to create a method of divination in a vacuum.

The first grew out of a game of patience, played with an ordinary pack of cards. David Hamblin, a professional counsellor and astrologer, decided to see whether he could devise a method of divination using the symbolism the cards already contained, and the sequence of the game, to provide a basis for interpretation. The card game is called "The Four Seasons" and involves building up the suits of cards in order, from King through Ace and upwards, according to the rules of dealing and laying out the cards. If any one suit can be completed from King through to Queen, then the patience is successful; this happens, apparently, about one time out of two.

David Hamblin found that if a question was posed before starting the game, he could make a divinatory judgement by the way the sequence proceeded, and whether it came to a conclusion. For instance, if he asked about the future of a certain project, he could judge how it would progress by the suits that were building up most rapidly. If the Heart suit was the first to be laid out, then this might indicate that the project would have emotional beginnings, and be carried along by good will, but if the suit of Spades then took over this would mean that a great deal of hard work would follow. The pace of the game could show the speed at which the project would progress, and the success or failure of the patience be related to the eventual outcome. These were just some of the guidelines he found effective. It was a system that he felt could have been developed further, and was proving effective in its readings, but as it had been set up as an experiment it was not taken to the final stages of definition.

The second system was devised, developed and marketed under the title of "Galgal: The Master Game". Galgal is a Hebrew term meaning "Wheels", and these wheels refer to the emblems on each card in the pack of fifty-six (see diagram). As in the previous example, the designers of Galgal drew on the notion of four suits of cards, but in this case the symbols on the cards are quite different.

The symbols have their origin in the Cabbalistic Tree of Life. The "Tree" is a stylised representation, consisting of ten circular points connected by straight-line "paths". The ten points are arranged in three vertical lines, known as the "three pillars" (see page 126). The Tree is a map of creation, defining the areas of body, personality, soul and spirit in man, and the active principles which govern and balance the universe. It has been applauded as one of the most universal "maps" available to mankind, since it can be related to just about any sphere of activity or knowledge – human, scientific, or religious.

In Galgal, different sections of the Tree have been taken and redrawn in circular form. The Cabbala is chiefly known as a Judaic system, though it may have had its roots in ancient Babylonia, and was adopted into the Christian world by the Renaissance philosophers. (It may be traced in the work of the painter William Blake and of the poet W. B. Yeats.) The Hebrew alphabet has twenty-two letters, and the Tree of Life has twenty-two paths – hence it is a natural operation to align the one with the other. There are different ways of doing this, but the creators of Galgal found that by following certain principles of ordering, the letters on the paths would then very easily form words when sections of the Tree containing three or more connected paths were taken. These sections then formed

An emblem from Galgal, the Master Game.

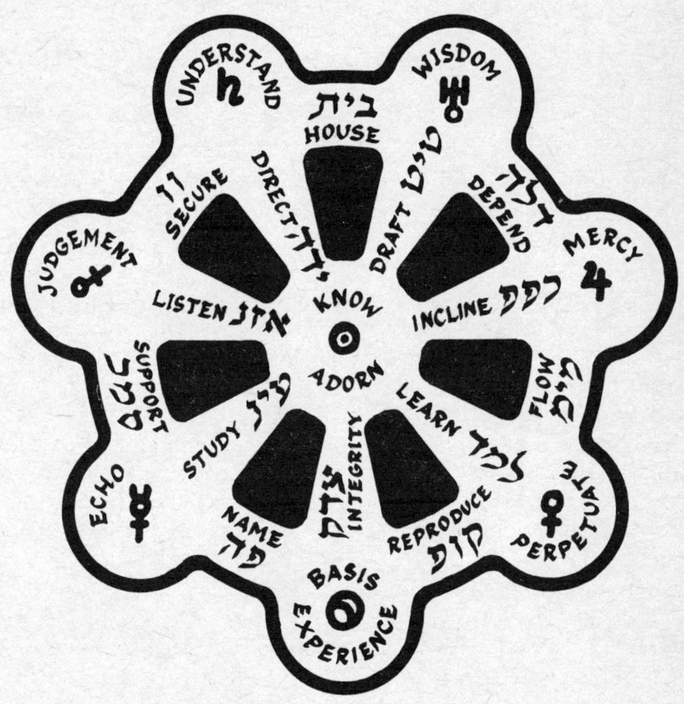

THE TREASURY † מד בו ספק

THE VICTOR → ובד מק פס

THE WARRIOR ♉ קמ דב וספ

THE HEART ⊗ דמ קפ סוב

Cabbalistic Tree of Life

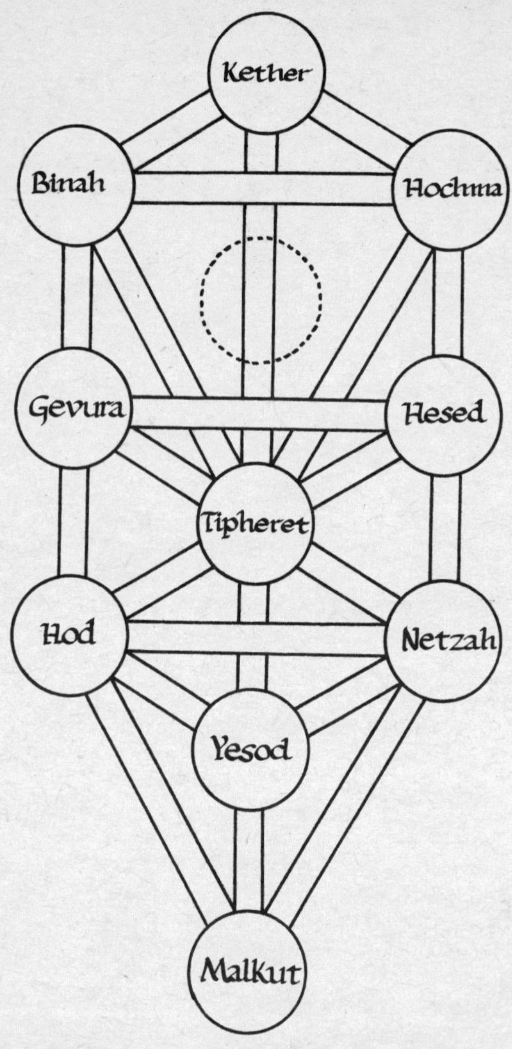

the emblems for Galgal, drawn in circular form and hence having more the appearance of "wheels". We have, for example, "The Myth", "The Drunkard", "The Well" and "Pride", "The Treasury" and "The Disciple". The interpretations for each card were then made by considering the name and the part of the Tree on which it was centred.

This is the essential framework of Galgal. It was a system that I witnessed in the making, and I was asked by its designers, W. G. Davies and G. Zur, to write a section for the accompanying booklet (Eddie Prevost and Cherry Gilchrist, *Galgal – The Master Game*, Scot o' the Covert, London, 1972). In this I described the way the cards should be laid out, in a method based upon the twelve astrological houses of life. Although Galgal is not widely known, it has been marketed and sold commercially, and used successfully by people who were not known to its originators, and who did not have knowledge of the Tree of Life. It stands in its own right as a divination system.

Thirdly, I should like to mention briefly a system in the making. This is known as "galactic astrology", the work of a group of astrologers in Manchester. Galactic astrology attempts to expand the existing sphere of astrology, giving it a framework which takes into account our relationship to the galaxy, rather than just to the solar system. The reason for the creation of this system lies in the fact that man is now exploring space. Our present astrology, as already mentioned, is entirely earth-based, and no ways of drawing up horoscopes satisfactorily for other points in the solar system or the galaxy yet exist.

To extend the scope of astrology, therefore, the galactic axis is used, based on the relationship of our solar system to the galactic centre. The greater circle which is then derived from this is divided, in galactic astrology, once again into twelve sections, as in conventional astrology, but each section is given a different archetype and description. These archetypes relate to the fundamental occupations of man (it will be remembered that the zodiac is a circle of animals!) and have titles such as "Trader", "Healer" and "Teacher". The focus of ordinary astrology is to describe the psychology of the individual in the natal horoscope. In galactic astrology, it is maintained, a greater sphere of reference is being used, and therefore the interpretation will come from a deeper level of meaning. Thus a "galactic" chart is said to relate to the laws of cause and effect governing individual lives, to the karmic element of destiny and the affiliations a person may have to other times, and to particular lines of work. It has been found especially illuminating to draw up galactic charts for men and women of creative genius – painters, poets, etc – whose outstanding ability is often not easily seen in the conventional natal chart.

Galactic astrology is a system in the making, but one that may

The Twelve Sigils

prove very useful as man becomes a voyager in space. It does make use of a set of twelve "sigils" – which are, as far as is known, a recent discovery of the twelve different forms that arise when six points, set in a circle, are joined. (See diagram.) They show the complete range of possibilities, when one continuous line is used to connect all six points without touching any point twice. Galactic astrology uses these sigils as a part of its symbolic correspondences, but they have arisen independently of galactic astrology and been the focus of research of a philosophical, mathematical and imaginative nature in various working groups.

These sigils are illustrated in diagram form, and, if the reader is so inclined, he or she is invited to study them and to see if a new divination system can be created from them. The sigils can be seen as images, or as dynamic processes. They can be related to each other through defining the ways in which one sigil turns into another through "swapping" a pair of points. This creates cycles of change. They can also be viewed as structured areas of space, similar to crystalline formations. As a set of symbols, they have great potential, only a little of which has been so far discovered.

Chapter 7

"The Truth about Time"

The title for this chapter has been chosen a little tongue-in-cheek. It would certainly be wishful thinking to assume that I could fulfil the aim it implies. Yet the ultimate questions about divination revolve around the principles of truth, time, and the operation of will: what is truth? what is time? and what is the nature of the will that governs them? Theologians and philosophers have battled over such questions for centuries, but the investigation of them is not the special privilege of an intellectual elite; it can soon be told through ordinary conversation that nearly everyone has his or her own ideas about whether there is such a thing as fate, what the nature of "reality" is, and whether we can use our power of choice or are the victims of circumstance.

In setting out some relevant views on these themes, both here and in earlier chapters, it is my intention to suggest ideas which may be helpful in expanding our everyday notions of the world; to draw upon theories from past and present which may also be illuminating; and to search for common ground among these in a way that will, hopefully, have meaning for us in our present culture. It is not my intention to examine every philosophy of divination that has ever been presented, and to make judgement upon these, or to suggest some particular structure as the model of absolute truth. Fundamental questions about divination are not going to produce final answers, and, indeed, we need to be able to ask them over and over again, to wrestle with their implications so that we create "answers" which are relevant for our own location in time and space.

Truth

In the classical and the Renaissance ages, a familiar saying was: "*Veritas filia temporis*", or: "Truth is the daughter of Time". Truth and Time were often personified together in a way that suggests bonds of love and respect between them. The Elizabethans, always pleased to take a fruitful conceit one stage further, identified the royal personage of Elizabeth I with "Truth" and saw her as a living embodiment of the principle. Among the pageants and emblems set up for her admiration upon royal tours is recorded one at Cheapside, where ". . . there were two hills, each with a tree on it, one withered to represent a 'decayed commonweale' the other green to represent a 'flourishing commonweale', and between the two came forth Truth and Time. The point of this was not lost on Elizabeth who is said to have cried, 'And Time hath brought me hither!' " (*English Emblem Books*, Rosemary Freeman). Many Elizabethan lute songs paid a double tribute to a personal love and to the sovereign in their imagery and a combined homage to love, Elizabeth and Truth is embedded in the beautiful text set by the composer John Dowland:

Time stands still with gazing on her face,
Stand still and gaze, for minutes, hours and years, to her give place:
All other things shall change, but she remains the same,
Till heavens changed have their course, and Time hath lost his name.
Cupid dothe hover up and down blinded with her fair eyes,
And Fortune captive at her feet contemn'd and conquer'd lies.

("Time Stands Still", *The Third Book of Songs*)

Truth was sometimes pictured unveiled in her nakedness by Time, who held a Sun or a mirror representing that which clears away all dark ignorance and cannot lie. In describing some of these historic images, my aim is to show that the ideas of Truth and Time had a poetic vitality, a mythical dimension which could be presented through emblems and symbols.* They were not just abstract concepts for the academics to argue over. And

*Acknowledgements to Anthony Rooley, whose research and lecture "Time Stands Still" have highlighted the combined symbolism of Truth and Time in Elizabethan culture and music.

if I could wish to accomplish anything in this present chapter, it would be to touch on the life of these principles and communicate this.

Truth, then, is a "product" of Time; in her most common classical representation, she is seen naked (as we speak of "the naked truth") but, by implication, she can appear in many garbs. Her clothing is an outward show – an adornment of beauty, practicality or decency, according to circumstance – for, in her essential self, Truth does not have this covering. Truth, at heart, is one, but may be glimpsed in countless different fashions.

This brings us back to divination, for the question: "Does divination work, and if so why?" may be answered in many different ways, each with its own measure of truth. An answer comes in some form, and whether that means in words, or through some other medium, it is a "dressed-up" form of truth. At different times and in different places we find particular types of dress more appealing, descriptive, or suggestive, according to our tastes and desires. We may sense and know "the naked truth" that lies beneath, but when it comes to defining and conveying that truth, it has to be done through an outer form. The forms in which truth appears are immensely variable, for those that could be comprehended by, let alone be useful to, Stone Age Man, must differ radically from those appreciated by Space Age Man.

It is certainly an interesting line of enquiry to look into the fashions that truth adopts. But to follow this further would be to veer away from the central topic of divination. What is relevant here is to emphasise that there are many different explanations as to how divination may work, and this will always be the case, since our personal, cultural and religious biases shape these explanations differently. Descriptions of truth are always interpretations; the diviners watching the leaping flames within the castle chamber interpret them through their own perceptions.

To make the point another way, an example can be taken from a course that I once gave on the symbolism and philosophy of astrology. All the participants were experienced astrologers, and many had delved quite deeply into philosophy, too. In one discussion session they were asked to consider a list of commonly-held views as to why astrology worked, and then to say which one they favoured and why. The list (by no means an exhaustive one) was, briefly:

1. That we are influenced by planetary rays.
2. That the law of synchronicity prevails – each moment in time having a character which is imprinted on everything born of that moment.
3. A hierarchical structuring of the cosmos means that the influence of the Divine Will reaches us via the intermediaries of the planets.
4. We measure astrology by the solar system because it has its own consciousness, parallel in its attributes to ours.
5. Greater and lesser unities are mirrored in one another; the macrocosm is reflected in the microcosm and vice versa.
6. Astrology is a created system, whereby the planets are outward tokens chosen to represent the elements of man's psyche.

The discussion was, to put it mildly, a heated one. The climate of the times, partly dictated by the current scientific world view, meant that number one was soon abandoned, and those with little sympathy for a Renaissance cosmos could not do with number 3. After historical and scientific reasons had demolished some of the proposals, it soon became obvious that personal experience and religious affinities were the factors which dictated one's choice. It also became apparent that passionate "reasoned" arguments for one particular theory had little influence on others of a different persuasion, since they had a similar measure of emotional commitment that they were not willing to abandon without a fight – and such a fight would not be won through "logic".

My main purpose in setting up this exercise was to try to show this very fact. We take a form of truth to our hearts because it serves a particular purpose – it "makes sense" to us because of our own framework of understanding, and disposition. This form of truth may allow us to extend our knowledge; it can be a vehicle for our own development, or for taking understanding to a deeper level. Recognising that there can be other forms of truth does not free us from the need to *use* our "own" form, for we all need such vehicles. However, seeing that different forms of truth are relative may open our eyes to the validity of other viewpoints, and may make us more able to help create new forms when the need arises. For example, "answer" number four on the list has particular appeal at the moment, as we are exploring the solar system through space flight, have a great interest in the "life" of the earth in terms of ecology and the cycles of nature, and so on and so forth. But if human beings are eventually born beyond the confines of the solar system, then astrology has to find a new form, or perish. If point 4 is taken for an absolute truth, then, by definition, astrology has no relevance beyond the solar system. Number one "truth" seems very out-dated at present. But what if science discovers an extremely subtle form of energy, creating planetary fields that embrace and affect us in equally subtle ways here on earth? Then, once again, this theory may find favour in a suitably re-vamped form.

This exercise was based on the assumption that astrology works, and this book is written around the premise that divination works. As I explained in the Introduction, I have not set out to "prove" that it works. The "naked truth" of divination is the personal discovery that it can and does work; assessing the way in which it works is the "dressed" truth. In my view, there is no single reasoned argument that will convince the sceptic that divination works. On the other hand, any of several philosophies, images or personal experience may lead to the understanding that divination can work if the individual is ready and receptive for that truth. To accept the principles of divination implies a willingness to know a greater sphere of existence than the personal, to acknowledge that there is more to life than that which can be weighed and measured by physical apparatus. It is a rare individual who never has any experience of this, but it is also common to ignore it, or to reason it away. Of course, reason is a useful tool; very often the fear is that if reason does not take total control we shall be at the mercy of fancies and wild imaginings, and lose hold of everyday reality. There are traps – the dark, empty corners of the castle – but imagination, in the proper sense of the word, has its own mode of reality, and emotions and intuition can sense and communicate in a way that reason cannot. We can train ourselves to balance out these different faculties, so that we do not lose the power of rational discrimination, but can decipher the messages of emotion and intuition too, which are often presented through images or sensations. Divination can assist that process by providing a ready-made framework of images that helps to give the process more objectivity.

Divination is by no means infallible. It is not always either "right" or "wrong"; sometimes it can provide knowledge of great significance, whereas at others its findings seem rather trivial. Sometimes it may seem to be right in general, but inaccurate in particular. The "truths" of divination's working in popular parlance are usually expected to be of the type: "Well, the card reader said to me that within a year I should come into some money and cross the water. Nonsense, I said. But she was right – Uncle George quarrelled with his daughter, then died and left me all his money so we went and had a holiday in Florida!" Certainly this kind of result does sometimes occur – though not as often as we might wish. But usually the truth conveyed through divination is more to be found in the quality of experience. The questioner may have the sense that the diviner has gone right to the heart of the matter enquired about, and is speaking with direct knowledge about it. The diviner may have the feeling that the normal barriers of communication have dissolved, and that he or she is speaking with knowledge that has authority, yet is not personal. Questioner or diviner or both may sense that there is truth coming through into this particular reading. The diviner focuses and interprets the seekings of the questioner through the medium of the divination system used. Both have to be ready and willing to take part in the transaction for it to be effective. It is a readiness to receive truth.

It would not be right to imply that the process of divination is usually a deep, mystical experience. Often it can be quite matter-of-fact in the way that it is conducted, although often, too, the impact can be strong and the diviner should be aware that if he or she touches on truth, it may produce a strong emotional reaction in the other person. Sometimes the truth of a reading may not be recognised by one or other till a much later date. It is the responsibility of the diviner to try to deliver the truth contained in a reading, even if it does not seem to accord with what his or her *personal* ideas of the truth may be.

Thus it is being stated that the truth of divination *has* to be sought on a personal basis. If there are experiences which one has acknowledged during one's life as "out of the ordinary", then divination no longer seems such a strange procedure. Most of us have experienced occasions when we have known who is going to be on the other end of the line when the phone rings, and have had dreams that have given us information which we could not have acquired by other means, or have heard a friend speak the very thought that was in our minds. Often the trademark of such experiences is that they seem eminently natural at the time – it is only afterwards that we suddenly realise the implications. Sometimes we may insist on explaining it all away, but the original experience is usually one of knowing it for truth in a quiet, certain and unconcerned way.

The models of *how* divination works, once one is past the hurdle of deciding that it *does* work, are varied according to the belief structure of the times and peoples amongst whom they originate. A common theme, however, seems to be acknowledging that there is another world, a greater sphere of knowledge into which we can pass. An American Indian woman shaman speaks thus:

> There is a world beyond ours, a world that is far away, nearby and invisible. And there it is where God lives, where the dead live, the spirits and the saints, a world where everything has already happened and everything is known. That world talks. It has a language of its own. I report what it says.
>
> (María Sabina in *Shamanic Voices*, ed. Joan Halifax, Pelican Books, 1980)

The poet and occultist W. B. Yeats identified this larger world as the "Anima Mundi", or world soul, in common with Platonic thought, and he perceived this to be the medium for suprapersonal knowledge and the receptacle for archetypal and mythical images, which often play a part in divination. He felt that he could move in and out of that realm, sometimes at will, sometimes triggered off by what he was reading or seeing. He described the experience:

I look at the strangers near as if I had known them all my life, and it seems strange that I cannot speak to them: everything fills me with affection, I have no longer any fears or needs; I do not even remember this happy mood must come to an end. It seems as if the vehicle had suddenly grown pure and far extended and so luminous that the images from *Anima Mundi* embodied there and drunk with that sweetness, would, like a country drunkard who has thrown a wisp into his own thatch, burn up time.

(*Per Amica Silentiae Lunae*, 1917)

This combination of self-forgetfulness and yet widened attention is often the experience of a person undertaking divination. One is aware of being right there within the moment, yet unaware of the passing of time.

The larger world that awaits us is sometimes viewed as another aspect of our identity. The psychologist C. G. Jung, whose own psychic experiences were numerous, labelled this the "collective unconscious", and stated that this is "common to all; it is the foundation of what the ancients called 'the sympathy of all things' ". He made this discovery early on in his own life; he felt that he had a dual nature:

Somewhere deep in the background I always knew that I was two persons. One was the son of my parents, who went to school and was less intelligent, attentive, hard-working, decent, and clean than many other boys. The other was grown up – old, in fact – sceptical, mistrustful, remote from the world of men, but close to nature, the earth, the sun, the moon, the weather, all living creatures, and above all close to the night, to dreams, and to whatever "God" worked directly in him. ... Beside his [the schoolboy's] world there existed another realm, like a temple in which anyone who entered was transformed and suddenly overpowered by a vision of the whole cosmos, so that he could only marvel and admire, forgetful of himself. Here lived the "Other", who knew God as a hidden, personal, and at the same time suprapersonal secret. Here nothing separated man from God; indeed, it was as though the human mind looked down upon Creation simultaneously with God.

(C. G. Jung, *Memories, Dreams, Reflections*, Collins and Routledge and Kegan Paul, 1963)

The ancients looked upon the realm from which divination arose as that of the gods. Xenophon sets out in his recollections of Socrates the sage's sensible distinction between using common sense and using divination:

But if the outcome of something was doubtful, he sent his friends to the oracle to find out whether or not this ought to be done. Those who wanted to take good care of their household or of the state, he said, needed divination in addition [to their expertise]. . . . You may marry a beautiful woman, but you do not know whether she will bring you grief; you may gain powerful connections in the state through your marriage, but you do not know whether you will be exiled because of them. If any man thinks that none of these pursuits is controlled by a divine force and that all of them depend on human reason, he must be mad. But it would also be mad to seek by divination something which men are allowed by the gods to learn by using their reason, to ask, for example: Is it better to hire an experienced coachman to drive my carriage or one who has no experience?. . . . This applies to everything that can be determined by counting, measuring, or weighing. To put such questions to the gods he considered an act of impiety. He said that we must learn what the gods have allowed us to achieve by learning, and that we must try to find out from them by means of divination what we, as human beings, cannot know for certain; the gods would give a clue to those who were in their favour.

(Quoted in *Arcana Mundi*, ed. Georg Luck, Johns Hopkins University Press, 1985)

The idea of oracles touching upon the kingdom of the gods was sometimes modified by putting particular oracles under the influence of "daemons". These lesser spirits were, interestingly enough, considered to have a limited lifespan. When the daemon died, then the life would leave the oracle. This implies a recognition that divination forms are a relative truth, not absolute nor immortal.

The theory that our knowledge derives from more than one source – for instance, from both the natural world and the divine, or from both reason and intuition, from the individual and the collective consciousness, is recurrent in the descriptions of how divination works. Francis Bacon echoes this concept with poetic impact in his *Advancement of Learning*:

The knowledge of man is as the waters, some descending from above, and some springing from beneath; the one informed by the light of nature, the other inspired by divine revelation.

Paracelsus, famous and eccentric doctor and philosopher of the sixteenth century, wrote in great detail of the types and operations of divination, and the source from which they derive their authority. He created his own terminology and his definitions are extremely complex, so that it is hard to present his arguments in brief. However, he saw man as partaking of the spirit of the starry heavens, and of thus being able to read celestial messages and discover their meanings and presages. He took his theories of the scale and interconnections of life into a wider context than that of divination by astrology or the like. He saw Nature as having a life of her own, with which man was also connected. "Nature," he said, "herself is a magus. If about to announce anything, she creates for herself messengers." Man may either understand natural portents and omens through his complete simplicity – as a child of nature, he may instinctively recognise some of these – or he may train himself with learning and skill to intentionally interpret the patterns of nature and the indications at the "starry" level of life. "The firmament foreknows all future things, nor does anything escape its knowledge, whether of things past or things present." (*Hermetic Astronomy*).

Drawing towards the end of this exploration of the nature of truth in relation to divination, I can summarise as follows. The presence of truth has to be recognised directly by the person concerned, rather than being proved through words, statistics, etc. Truth is of necessity clothed, and its clothing takes many forms which may strike us favourably or unfavourably according to personal, cultural and historical associations. But among the many descriptions and explanations of why divination works, there are certain common themes. The chief of these is that divination is the process of getting in touch with a source beyond our normal personal resources, a realm where knowledge beyond our individual knowledge can be discovered and brought into the forefront of consciousness. That source may be known in different ways – as divine, as collective consciousness, as the soul of the world or the life of Nature, or as all these.

Truth in divination is simple, just as Truth has been personified as naked simplicity. Very often one may experience that a divination reading is right in essence, but incorrect or irrelevant in detail. The specifics seem to come second to the general; that is to say, the core of truth that can become known through divination can be comprehended without all its particular manifestations being accurate. It is that core of truth that will actually convey meaning, rather than dozens of technicoloured particulars. The acknowledgement of truth has the power to change; truth is an active state of being.

My own suggested image of the truth of divination is set out in Chapter 1, as the castle which may be entered from the garden of the natural world, with its chamber where the fires of meaning may be contemplated. Throughout the book I have suggested ideas and analogies for considering particular aspects of divination. These have all been set out with the aim of stimulating the mind and imagination of the reader so that he or she may arrive at an understanding of the truth of divination in accordance with personal philosophies and beliefs. If the scope of these can be extended, so much the better.

Time

Although Time's daughter, Truth, takes pride of place in this chapter, I should like to give some space to looking at ideas of time as well. Divination claims to be able to move with a certain freedom in the context of time, to speak about what happened in the past, what is happening out of sight in the present, and what will happen in the future. Clearly there can be different models by which we understand time, as the science of relativity and quantum physics has shown. Our own experience of time can be subjective, according to the situation we find ourselves in; time may seem to go fast or slowly; time experienced in dreams is totally different from that of waking life. "Clock" time is an artificial measurement, chosen as the most convenient way of recording the passing moments; astronomically there are several ways of doing this. To "live in the past", "live in the moment" and "live in the future" are emotional realities, even if they have no physical foundation in fact. It is plain that we can comprehend time in different ways. If divination claims to provide methods by which we can move about freely in the space/time continuum, on what understanding of time is this claim based? After all, despite Einstein's findings, today is still today and tomorrow has not yet come!

Paradoxically, I think that the most useful understanding of time as it relates to divination is based on the reality that exists now, in this moment. The past and the future both depend on what is, here and now. What is "gathered up" by divination from the past, and what can be foreseen, both derive from the quality of life in the present. Strangely enough, this statement seems to suggest that the future is more knowable than the past, for, it may be argued, the past is all fixed and unalterable, whereas what may happen in the future may be quite reasonably inferred from what is going on in the present.

Let us take them in order: past, present and future. A divination question may frequently involve trying to find out what has already happened; readers may remember the heroic efforts of William Lilly to find out who had stolen his fish (pages 93–94)! In a character reading, the interpreter may often wish to comment on the significance of events that have happened in the past. Now, in human experience, the past may be recorded, but it is always recorded through interpretation. History books written by nations opposed in warfare may present quite different views of events. A child remembers events in ways that an adult does not. Our own memories are carefully edited, and change their shape with the passage of time. Who has not gone over an unsatisfactory conversation in the mind and re-scripted it? Those who keep diaries may be astonished to find on re-reading that a carefully worded description of an important day bears little relation to the significant incident as recalled a year or so later. This is inevitable; our past changes form in our minds as we change, grow and age.

Time and experience are inextricably linked. Cameras and tape recorders can take lasting impressions of a moment, but even photos and records are a two-dimensional impression of reality, and are created within the bounds of human perceptions. Thousands of different impressions of that reality could be created and held – either in the mind, or in concrete form. A dog cannot make sense of a photograph because it is an image made in human terms, made by a mechanism designed to capture impressions of the sort that human beings can recognise and make sense of. If there is a "greater mind", then its past, too, will be one of remembered impressions, a "created" rather than a completely objective past. Perhaps all our perceptions, images and emotions feed into a collective human memory.

In divination it seems that the knowledge that can be gleaned from the past is certainly more than that which the individual memory contains, but the volition of the individual question and the form of individual experience will create natural parameters to that which is received. Who I am, and what question I ask, will determine the type of answer that I find. The idea of a greater memory can work very much to advantage in divination, because it implies that we can obtain more information than that which is normally at our disposal, and yet it is likely to be relevant to our own state and needs. The limitations also become apparent, for if we try to seek information about events in the past with which we have no personal affinity, then any response at all that we get is likely, at best, to be heavily coloured by imagination.

Personally, I would not dismiss the idea that we can have affinities with past times and places with which we have had no direct contact in our own lifetime. But I would argue that even these affinities may change as we ourselves change. It is interesting to experiment by casting one's mind back through the centuries, following the thread from present to darkest past. Do you feel a response as you move back through particular periods of time? You may feel that you "belong there", or have some knowledge that tugs at the back of your mind, even if you can't quite bring it to the surface. But if you try the experiment in another two or three years, you may find that the responses are different and that you are homing in on different centuries entirely. Your own experiences, and state of being, may create different affinities as you travel through life.

This spells out the danger of divining "past lives" for other people, as some diviners are fond of doing. Such revelations may indeed strike a chord within the questioner's heart. But if he or she comes to believe in them too strongly, the identification can become a tie to the past which is cruelly hard to shake off when the person is ready to move forward in life. Indeed, reincarnation may have a reality – it is a complex subject, as the Buddhist scriptures emphatically point out. But even on the assumption that we all have many past lives, it is not necessarily helpful to have our emotions and attention focused on one or two of them. Certainly the Buddhist understanding of reincarnation is aimed at becoming free of the chains of the past, not more closely bound by them.

The concept of time as a kind of sequential film, in which the future is already scripted, shot, and ready on the reel to pass by our expectant gaze, is not a helpful one in the context of divination. It is more useful to think of knowledge of the past and sensations of the future being defined by our state of being in the present. We are not removed from the process of time; we help to shape it. As Francis Bacon says: "But man must know, that in this theater of man's life it is reserved only for God and angels to be lookers on." We can think of the present moment as a dot in space. This dot is at first sight a point on a line, the two sections of the line representing past and future. But then it is seen that the dot is at the centre of a series of concentric circles, which of course also pass through that line. The present moment, like a stone thrown into a pool, creates rippling circles that affect both past and future. Divination helps us to explore the nature of those circles, extending our knowledge beyond the normal perceptions of the dot of now, the known line of the past and the anticipated but unseen line of the future.

I have already broached the rather alarming notion that our knowledge of the past is not fixed, and that we can even affect the past through the present. Understanding that divination can reach into hidden territory of present and future then becomes almost simple! Going forward in time can be most clearly understood as the unfolding of the present moment. There is a chain of cause and effect, the operation of law, the working out of principle. If divination can penetrate to the level where this essential pattern is perceived, then the knowledge it conveys is also of the essence; the meaning of the present is grasped, and from that the relevance of the past and the consequences of the future. The details of events and their timing are likely to be of secondary importance. Some divination systems (such as horary astrology) are constructed to bring as much precision as possible to material predictions and the timing of events, but it is widely recognised that there is no guarantee of such accuracy, and that divination aims at the heart of the matter. Even horary astrology is founded on the "yes or no" principle, questions asked of it centring round dilemmas of success/failure, truth/falsity, growth/decay and so on. It aims first of all to tap the intrinsic nature of the matters enquired about and, while the details of "how, when and where" may well be picked up, they nonetheless revolve around this nucleus and derive from it.

Knowing the future, then, depends on the present. What is already in operation will have results. Plutarch stated this law quite simply, again seeing the significance of prediction as residing in the present moment:

> The god is a prophet, and the art of prophecy concerns the future as it results from the present and the past. There is nothing that comes into being without a cause, nothing that could not reasonably be predicted. Since the present follows the past and the future follows the present very closely, according to a constant process that leads from the beginning to the end, he who understands the natural connections and interrelationships of the causes with one another can also declare (Hom., Il. 1.70) "the present, the future and the past". Homer was right to place the present first, then the future, and then the past, for syllogism based on a hypothetical proposition has as its base that which is; for instance, "if this is, then this (other thing) has preceded it" or "if this is, then this (other thing) will be."
>
> (From *On the E at Delphi*, quoted in *Arcana Mundi*, ed. Georg Luck, Johns Hopkins University Press, 1985)

Some divination systems, such as the Tarot or the I Ching, will give a potential means for going straight into that essence of the present moment. Others have in-built concepts of timing, that help us to understand the probable progression of events according to principles which go beyond those governing the physical world. In astrology, for example, the principle of cycles is fundamental to the art of prediction. According to natural astronomical laws, we understand and anticipate the changing pattern of the seasons, which is due to the circling of the earth around the sun. According to astrological principles, we judge the patterns of individuals, and of nations, by the cycles of the planets and the moon as well, and extract knowledge from their complex interactions. One may take a person's horoscope (drawn up for the moment of birth), and judge, by seeing how Jupiter interacts with the planets in the natal chart as it moves on its twelve-year cycle round the zodiac, how the individual concerned will experience the Jupiter-type energies in his or her life at any given point in time. However, even here, in a divination system that has specific methods for plotting past, present and future, the exact way in which these influences will manifest is never certain.

In divination, it soon becomes clear that the barrier between internal and external events is a thin one. The image I have suggested, of concentric circles spreading out from a central point, with the axis of time running through them, can be still further defined by seeing the semi-circles on one side of the line as representing the internal, and the rest the external. They are a connected whole, and any movement or ripple will be common to both. When events come upon us suddenly, we may find it very hard at the time to understand why, but later we recognise that they had their own meaning as part of the life we were leading at the time. A road accident (the other person's fault, of course!) can bring about anything from temporary shock to serious injury, apparently unsought and undeserved. But many people who have suffered this see with hindsight that there were strong contributory factors originating in their own natures – common examples of these are that they were at the time looking for a fight, wanting something to happen, avoiding making crucial decisions, working too hard, etc, etc. And after a period of time such a traumatic event may even be seen as a blessing in disguise. It may not have been strictly *necessary* for the event to have taken that form – accidents are often a "last resort" when there is no other outlet for the energy – but it has served its purpose. As the I Ching hexagram "The Arousing" says:

Shock brings success.
Shock comes – oh, oh!
Laughing words – ha, ha!

The shock terrifies for a hundred miles,
And he does not let fall the sacrificial spoon and chalice.

(*The I Ching*, Richard Wilhelm translation, Routledge and Kegan Paul, 1951)

We work in the present moment, but we can, through divination, move to a perspective where the connections between past, present and future are more clearly seen. As we move to this viewpoint, there is less clutter of detail and the principles at work become more apparent. A question asked through divination strikes a note, and answering resonances arise. These may sound not only from the immediate present, but from times gone, times to come, and also from the unseen reaches of the present itself. Divination helps to provide a medium for such resonances to be heard and recorded.

Will

The wise man rules Nature, not Nature the wise man. For the same reason we can accomplish more than the stars. In us, then, should abound so great a wisdom that we shall thereby control all things, not only firmamental virtues, but also living animals which yet are much stronger than man. The will of man extends over the depth of the sea and the height of the firmament.

(Paracelsus, *Hermetic Astronomy*)

Practising divination without keeping in mind the element of will reduces it to a mechanical level. It implies that the film is made, the reels are going round, and all we have to do is to sit back and wait for the pictures to come up on the screen. The best divination can do under such circumstances is to give us some sneak previews.

I have suggested that the significance of the past and the events of the future are bound up with our state of being in the present moment. From this follows the thought that if we choose to change our state, then past and future will also change in accordance with it.

To a large extent, as I have already suggested, the past is composed of images and memories. We live by these; in a mundane sense, we sit down upon a chair because we *remember* that it is a chair, designed for the weight and shape of the human body. Our memories contain thought and feeling, which continue to dictate many of our current actions. Through deliberate forms of work, such as dream-work, psychotherapy, or meditation, one may find that certain powerful memories begin to lose their hold. (Certainly this can also come with age and wisdom too!) We make judgements as we store away our impressions in the memory; if we see a parent as stern and threatening, then usually we will continue to stockpile memories that uphold this view. Or, at least, these will be the ones most readily available, the ones that carry on sustaining our image and judgement of that person. If a wider view develops, then the threat may disappear, the parent seen as bad-tempered but not all-powerful, unkind at times, but human and caring too. Other memories may start to emerge, which in their turn sustain this broader, more realistic portrait. We view the past differently, and if we remember it differently, it becomes another past to us, and shapes our present actions in a different way. In certain cases divination can help to give the wider view of the past, an insight into its structure and patterns of cause and effect, which helps us to be less enslaved by them.

Changing the present is easier to see; as a simple, everyday example, imagine a situation that is getting more and more tense and irritating. It could be at work, in the supermarket, travelling in the rush hour, or during peak demand time in the heart of the family – everything people do or say only adds to the aggravation. As things stand, the consequences are bound to be unpleasant – quarrelling, exhaustion, or whatever. But if one can drop the annoyance and even see the humour of the situation, then, magically, it loses its hold. The tiredness or difficulty don't entirely fade, but they are features of the situation, rather than enemies to be battled with. The consequences will then be different. What has happened is a change of state so that reactions which were dictating future actions and responses have ceased to prevail. This example is not given as a suggestion that we should laugh our way through life, come what may! But it indicates that we do have choice, and that our future depends upon the choices we make in the present. What course we choose, and why we choose it are complex issues – but choose we do.

Paracelsus implies that we can change the level of the will operating, and that rather than being totally subject to the influences of the natural world we can become responsible for our own lives. In divination, will comes into being when the questioner formulates his enquiry and states himself willing to listen to the answer. The diviner summons will through putting aside the cares and concerns of the moment to give full attention to the working of the system. Both questioner and diviner are willing to step beyond the bounds of normal thought processes. This might sound self-evident, but it is crucial. A half-hearted approach to divination from either party often results in lukewarm results – too generalised, or just plain off the mark. If the will to seek knowledge is not present, nothing of any consequence will be learnt.

Will should not be confused with force. It is quiet, colourless, and may often go unobserved. It is capable of dissolving apparently insurmountable difficulties, and creating effects way beyond the present. On the other hand, it does not and cannot flout natural law; rather, it uses it to advantage. So we cannot stop the planets in their courses: their cycles will continue, interacting with our horoscopes and giving astrologers material from which to make projections into the future. But if we have learnt how to handle some of the difficulties, and indeed gifts, that these cycles bring us, then they can be used as agents of transformation. Heredity, culture, personal make-up are all active features in our lives, but we have a measure of choice as to how we shape those features.

The question: "Why should the shuffling of cards or the casting of stones bring out any meaningful information?" is certainly relevant here. In themselves, they do not. What is happening in divination is that the will to seek for knowledge has been set in motion, and this will is capable of arranging things quite efficiently so that the relevant pictures, patterns, hexagrams, or whatever, will be revealed. Divination opens the way into a wider sphere of knowledge; entering into it through personal will, we may discover the existence and intent of greater wills than our own. Thus we may come to know the will of nature, the will of a nation, the will of the moment – and, dare I say it, the divine will which is the unity of all these, containing them, being the sum of them, the first and last.

Through divination we aspire to knowledge. Each person will have different horizons, different expectations. There is no such thing as the all-embracing answer, for who we are, and the systems we work with, will temper the answers that we seek for ourselves and for others. But divination gives us the chance to go further into the realm of knowledge, to perceive order in confusion and to sense meaning in the working out of our lives. What we do with that knowledge is then up to us.

SOME SUGGESTED READING

R. A. Gilbert, *The Golden Dawn: Twilight of the Magicians*, Aquarian Press, 1983

Cherry Gilchrist, *Alchemy: The Great Work*, Aquarian Press, 1984

Tom Graves, *Dowsing: techniques and applications*, Turnstone Books, 1976

Joan Halifax, ed., *Shamanic Voices*, Pelican Books, 1980

C. P. Hargrave, *A History of Playing Cards*, Dover, 1966

Michael Howard, *The Wisdom of the Runes*, Rider, 1985

Paul Huson, *The Devil's Picture Book* (a study of the Tarot), Abacus, 1972

Eve Jackson, *Astrology: a psychological approach*, Dryad Press, 1987

C. G. Jung, *Memories, Dreams, Reflections*, Collins and Routledge and Kegan Paul, 1963

C. G. Jung, *Synchronicity: An Acausal Connecting Principle*, Routledge and Kegan Paul, 1972

Georg Luck, ed., *Arcana Mundi: Magic and Occult Influence in the Greek and Roman Worlds*, Johns Hopkins University Press, 1985

Stephen Skinner, *The Living Earth Manual of Feng-Shui*, Routledge and Kegan Paul, 1982

Lyn Webster, *Dream-work: guide to the midnight city*, Dryad Press, 1987

Richard Wilhelm, trans., *The I Ching or Book of Changes*, Routledge and Kegan Paul, 1951

Compass of Mind

Astrology

a psychological approach

Eve Jackson

A psychological approach to astrology is interested in people rather than events, and views people as essentially psychological beings, with a capacity to influence as well as be influenced by circumstances.

In this broad introduction to astrology Eve Jackson explains how the symbolic language came into being and outlines some of the theories that have been put forward on how astrology works. She discusses the value of astrology today as a tool for psychological insights and shows how the horoscope can be used as an aid to personal growth. A chapter on new planets, looking at the circumstances and effects of their discovery, includes some original research on the recently discovered planetoid, Chiron. The book then considers the question of fate and free will, concluding that there is a kind of freedom in an acceptance of our limitations. The final chapter discusses astrological counselling, and other uses of astrology in modern times.

Eve Jackson is an astrologer and psychotherapeutic counsellor. Her first book, *Jupiter*, was published by The Aquarian Press in 1986.

Compass of Mind

Dream-work

guide to the midnight city

Lyn Webster

Working with dreams is only of value if it changes your waking life for the better. The aim is to make a relationship between the conscious and the unconscious mind which is beneficial to both—so that the consciousness has a much wider field of perception and the unconscious becomes organised to some degree.

Using a wealth of absorbing and intriguing examples from already published accounts and from her own experience and that of fellow-dream-workers, Lyn Webster explains what dream-work is and how it has been practised from classical times to the present, for healing, for self-development and as a means for contacting the creative within us. She details the pleasures and pitfalls of lucid dreaming, discusses true dreaming, which tells us something about the future, and looks at examples of "big dreams" which give an intimation of Truth. Advice is included on how to run a dream-group and on techniques which can be used for working with dreams.

Lyn Webster is a television producer/director and writer. She has kept a dream diary for twenty years, has run a dream-group and used dream-work in her own creative writing. Her first novel, *The Illumination of Alice J. Cunningham*, was published in 1987.

Compass of Mind

Meditation

and the creative imperative

Lucy Oliver

Different forms of meditation express their aims in different ways, ranging from relaxation to enlightenment or Union with the Divine, but there is a psychological process which is common to all forms. This book is a study of that basic process which is initiated when someone seriously begins to learn meditation in any tradition or with any technique.

The three most obvious results of meditation could be summarised as calmness, power and insight, representing refinement and development in the three levels of being—physical, emotional and intellectual. These three levels of being and the progress of meditation are reflected in the structure of the book. The earlier chapters outline the principles involved in acquiring the skill of meditation; the basic techniques and how they work; and how meditation relates to daily life. The second part explores the ways in which meditation affects emotional life, and the relationship of religion and meditation. The third, which will expand in meaning as the meditator's own experience deepens, deals with the way in which sustained meditation brings about a conceptual re-ordering and unfolds the creativity which characterises being human.

Lucy Oliver was born in Australia and moved to the UK in 1972. She was trained in the Saros tradition and has taught meditation for over six years.

For further information about "Compass of Mind" books, please write to Dryad Press Ltd, 8 Cavendish Square, London W1M 0AJ.

INDEX

Agrippa, Cornelius, 15, 40, 49, 50
alchemy, 21, 56–8, 66, 114
Anahita, 76
animals, divining through, 21, 24, 26, 38, 39, 42, 51, 118
"Anima Mundi", 136–7
Apollo, 20, 84, 95, 96, 103
  of Corope (oracle of), 103–4
archetype (definition of), 119
Assurbanipal, library of, 17
astrology, 14, 16, 19, 21, 25–6, 27, 30, 32, 43–6, 82, 90–2, 108, 112, 115–16, 118, 120, 122, 144–5
  galactic, 127–9
  horary, 13, 43, 82, 87–8, 144
  horoscope in, 25–6
    houses of, 45, 46, 82, 127
  philosophy of, 132–3
  planets in, 26, 44, 45–6, 100, 145
  zodiac in, 26, 32, 45, 122

Bacon, Francis, 138–9, 143
Bible, use of in divination, 24
birds, divination through calls and movements of, 11, 21, 24, 36, 38, 39–41, 42, 116, 118
Blake, William, 124

Cabbala, 61, 79, 124–7
cardinal virtues, 69
cards, playing, 24, 53, 59, 120
  patience game, divinatory, 123–4 (*see also* Tarot)
"Castle of Divination", 9–10
"Chime Child", 106
clairvoyance, 13, 19, 20 (*see also* psychism)
"collective consciousness", 55–9, 137, 139
crystal-gazing, 23
cycles, 20, 23, 25–6, 63, 100–102, 144–5, 148

"daemons", 138
Delphic oracle, 11, 13, 20, 27, 95–7, 103
  priestesses of, 11, 20, 84, 95, 96, 100, 103, 104
divination
  (*see* separate systems of divination, e.g. Tarot *and* media used for divination, e.g. birds)
  and magic, 18–19
  and science, 20–1, 43, 47
  and therapy, 113
  at:
    Christmas, 20, 85
    Easter, 25
    Hallowe'en, 25, 85–6
    Lent, 101
    May Day, 25
    Midsummer's Eve, 86
    New Year, 18–19, 25

divination—*cont.*
by:
children, 8, 36, 42–3, 86, 105–6
community, 16, 85–6
definition of, 11
false, 41–2
for:
character-reading, 14–15
guilt, determination of, 17–18, 24
history of, 11–12
in:
ancient Greece, 16, 90 (*see also* Delphic oracle)
ancient Rome, 17, 18–19, 85
Babylonia, 11, 17
Britain – Anglo-Saxon, 102
Celtic, 11, 40–1
during reign of Elizabeth I, 15, 85
during 17th century, 13, 25, 92–5
Greenland, 12
Lapland, 12
Thailand, 19, 47
rituals of, 8, 14, 20, 99, 103–4, 109
rules of – need for flexibility in, 99–100
that prevent judgement, 87–8
systems, choice of, 107, 108–9
creation of, 114–29
timing of, 8, 100–103 (*see also* time)
diviner, relationship with querent, 14, 81, 109–11, 112–13
responsibilities of, 9, 27, 82–4, 86, 98, 109–13
divining for water, hidden substances, 8, 15–16, 28–9, 88, 89 (*see also* dowsing)
from maps, 16, 29
divining rod, 5, 27
Dowland, John, 131
dowsing, 15–16, 24, 27–9, 88–9, 108 (*see also* divining for water, hidden substances)
dreams, 11, 12, 22, 24, 49–52, 58

eclipses, 11, 24, 46
elements (earth, water, fire, air), 23, 30, 33, 59, 117, 118
ether, 121
Elizabeth I, Queen of England, 131
entrail-reading, 17
Evangelists, the Four, 79

face-reading, 46–7
fate, aversion of, 19
Fortuna (goddess Fortune), 70, 131
Freya, 12

"Galgal", 124–27
"Gematria", 52
Geomancy, 30–2
Chinese, 37
"The Golden Dawn", 59–60

Hebrew alphabet, 52, 61
hexagrams (of I Ching), 33–6, 87
human body, divinatory readings based on, 46–9

I Ching (Chinese Book of Changes), 18, 30, 33–6, 87, 144, 145–6
Ishtar, 76

Jung, C. G., 18, 42, 55, 58, 137

"Katarche", 91

Leto, 96
ley lines, 37
Lilly, William, 92–5, 99, 100, 141
lots, drawing of, 17–18

Macbeth, 96
Macedon, Philip of, 96–7
microcosm, concept of, 114–16, 133
"Mistress of the Beasts", 71
Mithraism, 77
moon, phases of, 102
"morphic resonance", 55

nature, as basis for divination, 19, 36, 38–42, 115, 139
number, 10, 11, 36, 52, 116–18
  binary, 27–36, 53, 88, 117
numerology, 9, 52–3, 107

Odin, 72

palmistry, 9, 14, 27, 47–9, 82, 90, 108, 116
Paracelsus, 19–20, 139, 146, 148
pendulum, 15, 24, 27, 29, 88
phrenology, 47
psychism, 41, 104–7 (*see also* clairvoyance)
psychological imbalance, 41–2
psychology, 23, 41, 43, 47, 51, 58
psychometry, 14, 108
Pythia, *see* Delphic oracle, priestesses of

reincarnation, 142–3
runes, reading of, 53

sacrifices, animal, 17, 25, 103
St Francis, 41
shamanism, 12, 41, 49, 72, 104
Sheldrake, Rupert, 55
sigils, the twelve, 128–9
Socrates, 58, 138
sun, cult of, 77–8
supernatural, definition of, 11
symbols, use of, 10, 16, 36–8, 52, 53, 118–21
  in alchemy, 57–8
  in Tarot, 60–2
synchronicity, 42, 133

Tarot, the, 16, 27, 53, 54–80, 82, 86, 87, 90, 107, 108, 117, 118, 120, 144
tea-leaf reading, 24
time, concept and significance of, 7, 8, 25–6, 48–9, 82, 130, 140–6 (*see also* divination, timing of)
"Tree of Life", 124–7
truth
  definition of in divination, 131–40
  symbolic representation of, 131–2

weather, 15, 20, 24, 38, 42
will, 13, 146–9
witchcraft, 17, 86

Yeats, W. B., 50, 61, 124, 136–7